S E L F -
DEFENSE
W O M E N
for

SELF-DEFENSE for WOMEN

TECHNIQUES TO GET YOU HOME SAFELY

Elizabeth Pennell

Adams Media Corporation
Holbrook, Massachusetts

Published by
Adams Media Corporation
260 Center Street, Holbrook, MA 02343
www.adamsmedia.com

ISBN: 1-58062-340-9

Printed in the United States

J I H G F E D C B A

Library of Congress Cataloging-in-Publication Data
Pennell, Elizabeth.
Self-defense for women / by Elizabeth Pennell.
p.   cm.
Includes index.
ISBN 1-58062-340-9
1. Self-defense for women—Handbooks, manuals, etc. I. Title.
GV1111.5.p45   2000
613.6'6'082—dc21   99-088320

Illustrated by Elizabeth S. Pennell

This book is available at quantity discounts for bulk purchases.
For information, call 1-800-872-5627.

Acknowledgments

Any technical errors in this book are exclusively mine.

This book is dedicated above all to my teacher, Master Dave Leggeri, eighth-degree black belt in Shaolin Kempo Karate. Dave combines extraordinary skill with true humility, and is a shining example of all that is best in the martial arts.

This book is also dedicated to Susan Vigorito, my workout partner, advisor, and friend;

To Mike Vasicek, who keeps me humble;

And to John Deprato, with love and thanks.

Warning

The activities described in this book may be too strenuous or dangerous for some people and the reader should consult a physician before engaging in them. **Also,** the self-defense techniques described in this book can cause severe injury to others. They should be used only in emergency situations and for the purpose of self defense, except as directed for the purpose of practicing the techniques.

Contents

LESSON ONE:
THE BASICS

LESSON TWO:
HELLO, FLOOR

LESSON THREE:
YEOWCH!

LESSON FOUR:
LET GO!

LESSON FIVE:
CLUB DEFENSE

LESSON SIX:
KNIVES, GUNS, AND CLOSING WORDS

Preface

Why would anyone write a handbook on how to cause injury to other people? Won't the "bad guys" among us steal their own copies and learn the same things?

The bad guys are bad guys because they lack the brains, the nerve, the energy, and the will to participate in the world under the rules that govern responsible human interaction. Snatching a gold necklace takes a moment. Earning the money to buy the same necklace takes days or weeks. The bad guys will choose the easy way.

It is not easy to become good at defending yourself. It will take perseverance and diligent effort. If you read this handbook once, you might get the occasional chuckle and maybe even a fact or two. That's as far as the bad guys will get. If they were constitutionally capable of getting further, then they would not be bad guys. You can get further.

Find a partner. In the book, we use "he" for partner, but obviously a teenage or adult woman would work just as well. Set aside time every week to practice. Without practice, and lots of it, this book is only a useful self-defense tool if you hit somebody with it.

Lesson One

THE
BASICS

Lesson One

LEARNING TO FIGHT

All around you, every day, things change. Spring turns to summer. The kids get taller by the minute. Last year's computer is this year's paperweight. Cars get to look more and more like medication. (I'm sure you've all seen the new Buick Suppository.)

The human animal, however, has been engineered the same way for millennia. Oh, our foreheads don't slope quite as much anymore, and our knuckles aren't dragging on the ground as we walk, but when Ogla was attacked by Nibog in the primeval jungle and she kicked him in the knees and then bashed his head in with a rock, it worked for her as well as it would work for you. Of course, in the Neanderthal era, this did not lead to Phase Two, the Messy Lawsuit.

There is nothing esoteric about self-defense. There is a specific set of skills that will help you in any situation where you are forced to confront other humanoid bipeds who are bent on doing you bodily harm. The technology of war has changed; we get better and better at destroying people from greater and greater distances, in horrible ways. But when it comes down to you in an alley with a mugger, the same skills will serve you that worked in Shakespeare's day. These skills will work for anybody who is potentially the victim of aggression; they are not dependent on—nor limited by—gender, age, or size.

1. You need to know how to hit and kick. "You hit like a girl" only means that no one has showed you how to do it. Anyone can learn the right way to hit, just the way anyone can learn to tie shoes.
2. You need to know where the bad guy is vulnerable, so that you can hit and kick effectively. Punching the baddie in the upper arm does not have the same stopping power as punching him in the nose.

3. You need to learn how to recognize an attack, and how to block or redirect it.
4. You need to know how to fall down without getting hurt, so that you are ready and willing to fight from the floor.
5. You need to know how to fight from the floor; just because you are down does not mean that you are out.
6. You need to learn how to disrupt the attacker's balance, and how to keep your own.
7. You need to learn how to manipulate and lock joints so that even if you are much smaller than your attacker, you can control him.
8. You need to familiarize yourself with all the weapons at your disposal, including your fingers, fists, elbows, knees, feet, teeth, and nails, along with balance, momentum, speed, and surprise.
9. You need to learn how to stay calm and focused in a fight.

These are all skills that you can acquire with information and practice. This handbook will give you the former, and suggestions for how to go about the latter. Your part is to supply the energy, determination, and time.

Once you know *how* to fight, and feel comfortable that you are pretty good at it, you need to learn *when* to fight, so that you do not throw yourself heedlessly into battle at the slightest provocation. Fighting is bad. Getting hurt sucks. Causing harm to other people, even bad guys, sucks too. No matter how great it feels at the moment, it doesn't feel good a week later, at four in the morning when you can't sleep.

Once you commit to a fight, someone is going to get hurt. Always choose not to fight when this is one of your options.

A Word on Practicing

At some point, you'll want to get some real-world feedback, and chances are you will have some burly male friend who is willing to play attacker and let you practice. Then, using a whole lot of muscle—because generally he'll have more of that than you do (welcome to Biology 101)—he will try to show you that your techniques don't *really* work. I don't know why men, especially large men, feel the need to do this, but if yours doesn't, he's a rare bird. It's just some weird part of the human condition.

The key is: Don't believe him. The problem with practicing on someone you like is that technique is often predicated on the fact that you are hurting your attacker, which I hope you are not willing to do to your helpful bud. You can stop an attacker by kicking his knee into matchsticks, or driving your thumb into his eye. You are not going to do either of these things to good old Jimbo. You will have to use your intellect and your imagination when you practice, or you will have to administer enough pain to get Jimbo to let go, which may hurt his feelings too. Up to you. Just don't get discouraged if you are unable to immediately beat up all your friends and relatives. Self-defense is not a parlor trick, and the real world is vastly different from the practice arena.

THE LEGAL THING

This book does not discuss right, wrong, legality, or morality. It's up to you to use your best judgment to choose what you do in any given situation. There is no boilerplate set of rules. I can't promise you that you won't get in trouble for hurting someone who attacks you. The best advice I can offer is to tell you to do only what is necessary so that you get home safely. This the goal of self-defense. It is *not* up to you to see that the bad guy gets punished.

If someone is verbally harassing you, any physical response is overreaction, no matter how provoked you may be. However, if some guy grabs you, throws you on the floor, and jumps on top of you, I want you to be able to leave him in gasping, disabled disarray as you sprint for safety.

I'd like you to think about the idea of creating a window of opportunity through which you can make a speedy exit. It is never your mission to see that the bad guy gets what is coming to him. It is only your job to create the window and leave. Maybe the law will administer justice (and maybe not). Maybe justice will be served in the hereafter. Maybe the bad guy will simply get away with what he does. It's not your problem; you're not the law. If you got home safely, you did your job.

THREE KINDS OF SELF-DEFENSE SITUATIONS

Miscommunication

This happens when you think you are saying "no" but he hears "yes." The situation is complicated when you have some sort of cross-reference for your attacker. "It's only George," you think, "and he's Ethel's brother-in-law, and what if they talk about me behind my back? And of course, he wouldn't do anything really bad, I mean, I know him." Communication is a funny thing, especially between the sexes. You hear "no" coming out of your mouth, but he sees (and hears) what he wants to see. (This is not because he is malicious or stupid; it is because he is human.) If you have been drinking together all evening, and you have permitted a certain amount of intimate contact, and you're not being obviously rude, then no matter what you are saying, he may be hearing, "please, convince me to say yes."

At some point, however, you realize that the situation has gotten out of control. You may reach this conclusion before anything unpleasant has happened. You move to get up, and he casually reaches out and pulls you back down. He's still smiling, it's all good fun, but . . . "Uh-oh," you think. If you are paying attention to your gut, you get that uneasy feeling somewhere below your ribcage. (The feeling you used to get before you went to the dentist to have a cavity filled, remember?)

If you're getting that uh-oh feeling, it's time to create the window and scram, even if you're worried that you might look stupid. It is always better to look stupid than to get hurt.

There are several ways to create the window. You may not want to provoke the situation further by being overt ("Unhand me you brute"). Direct confrontation may have the effect of escalating matters. However, saying, "Excuse me, I feel really bad, I think I'm going to throw up!" puts a real damper on things, especially if, like my children, you have the knack for barfing on demand.

Such stratagems are not always likely to work, but they're worth a try before segueing into the Clumsy Me routine: the passionate caress that turns into an inadvertent thumb in the eye. That incidental head butt to the nose, the high heel to the instep, the swift knee to the nuts, the elbow to the solar plexus. "Oh, I'm soooooo sorry, I'm such a dork!" you murmur, as you exit gracefully on a wave of apologies.

If you don't realize until past this stage that things are out of hand, you will have to learn to fight nasty. We'll get to that in detail; it's mostly what this book is about. Don't worry, you don't have to be strong to fight nasty. You are plenty strong enough.

Random Disaster

This is what happens when you are in the wrong place at the wrong time. You are the person on the sidewalk when the junkie needs his next fix. You are the next passerby when the gang decides it's time to cause some trouble. You just happen to look like the mugger's ex-wife who just took him to court to get some child support, which is why he is out mugging passersby.

The first piece of advice is: Don't be there. Avoiding dangerous spots is part of "The Don't Be Stupid Lecture Notes," coming up next.

But sometimes you do all the right things (stay out of dark alleys, blah blah) and random disaster finds you anyway. I was once standing at the cash register of my local health food store when a guy came in, just a regular guy on a regular afternoon, and the next thing I knew he had me by the arm, had a gun pressed into my ribs, and was telling the cashier to empty the register and not try anything funny. By pure good fortune (and total pants-wetting fear) I had the wits to stay quiet. Television and the movies have inured us to violence in a way that came in handy at that point; I kept looking out the window waiting for Starsky and Hutch to ride up. (This lets you know how long ago this occurred.) When the robber finally threw me down on the floor and told me to stay down while he left, I kept wondering what it would feel like if he decided to shoot me while I lay there, to delay pursuit.

See, your brain doesn't always shut off in a panicky situation; sometimes it goes into such overdrive that you freeze. And sometimes freezing is your best option. We are NOT going to administer justice. All we want is to get home safely. (Everybody! All together!)

You should give some thought to what you would fight for. I didn't care to fight for the health food store's money. If the guy had been holding a gun to my kid's head (or my dog, or your kid, or anybody small and helpless—or, in my dog's case, unbelievably stupid) I would fight. Never fight for something as replaceable as money. Hand over your wallet, your car keys, your engagement ring.

At about this same era in my life, I was also successfully mugged on the way home from work. This was a successful mugging in that the bad guys got what they wanted—my stuff—and I got to walk away undamaged. That time it was, in a sense, my fault. Actually, this is incorrect. When you have been victimized by violence, it is NEVER YOUR FAULT. It is the fault of the stupid sonofabitch who made the choice to attack you. It isn't society's fault, it isn't his parents' fault, it isn't anybody's fault but his. Everybody makes choices, and as long as you didn't go out there and choose to get attacked ("Hey, fella, I'm awful bored, how about you pull out a knife and take all my stuff?") then it is *not* your fault if you got mugged.

In any case, I digress. What I should have said is, I broke the rules. I walked the same way home every night. I didn't stay on the well-lit street. I took the same shortcut through the parking lot at the same time every night. So, duh, one day two guys came walking up to me and damned if they didn't stick a gun into those very same ribs.

I was carrying shopping bags. They only contained groceries but they were fancy plastic shopping bags from the gourmet store, so they were deceptive—regular grocery bags masquerading as department store wannabes, appearing to be full of designer dresses and expensive perfume.

Guy A does the grab-biceps, jab-gun routine, and Guy B says, "Gimme your bags."

By now I'm an old pro at this mugging thing, so I'm completely relaxed. I say, "Come on, let me at least keep the yogurt, I have nothing in the house for dinner!"

The guy looks at me like I'm stupid. (He was right.) "Lady," he says, *"do you want to get shot for some yogurt?"*

So think of that question when you are confronted by the bad guys. Do I want to die for some stupid green paper? Do I want to spend weeks in the hospital with tubes protruding from my orifices for the chance to hang on to some piece of yellow metal or my lovely Rolex watch? Do I want to never throw a tennis ball for my dog again, never go to the beach again, just to save myself a trip back to the store? DO I WANT TO GET SHOT FOR SOME YOGURT?

You get my drift.

Stalking

The final kind of self-defense situation is stalking. Stalking is when the bad guy is out there looking for you personally and specifically, for whatever BB of a reason is rattling around in the tin can of his psycho head. Many seemingly regular people are a couple cans short of a six-pack. But you don't know until you pop the top on number five and, much to your surprise and dismay, the sucker is empty.

So you broke up with that nice man you were dating for a year or so. You were ready to settle and have kids, he was stuck on the fence, whatever reason, it just didn't work out. You never felt you were on the same page. You were Elaine, he was Roger, and Dave Barry was writing the book.

You go out a couple days later and your tires are slashed. Bad luck, you say, thinking again that it's about time you moved out of the city. Then you come home one night and someone's dog has actually had the temerity to come right up and make a mess on your porch. More bad luck.

If your bells don't start ringing real loud and quick about now, you should have them checked.

Whenever something has happened in your life that has the potential to generate strong emotions, you should be extra wary. You beat out someone for a promotion, you broke up with a boyfriend, you got into an argument with the guy who delivers the Chinese food (tip: order from a new place, this guy has control over what goes into your mouth). And don't even think about road rage. You are driving around in a big expensive box WITH AN IDENTIFYING NUMBER ON IT. Don't think you can be a jerk with impunity—the guy you cut off and to whom you cheerfully flip the bird could be a complete and total whacko. You just don't know. It is simply not smart to crash through life, pissing people off heedlessly as you go.

And you just don't know what will set somebody off, or who has that scary dark place inside his head that makes it seem okay to stalk somebody.

So, if you think you might have reason to be extra cautious, don't hesitate to do so. You might even read "The Don't Be Stupid Lecture Notes" twice.

THE DON'T BE STUPID LECTURE NOTES

You've all heard it: The Don't Be Stupid Lecture. I summarize the high points here just because even though you've all heard it, you don't seem to be exactly LISTENING to it. Yes, I mean you.

The best way to defend yourself is to be the least opportune person to mug. The mugger doesn't just cry out "The curse has come upon me!" and spring on the nearest person. He watches, waits, and chooses.

Think about this. The mugger is not a brave person, or he would not be victimizing others. He is not an energetic person, or he would have a job and show up at work regularly and have some money and not need to be out there mugging YOU. He's not particularly bright, ditto.

Ergo you must make good choices. If you look like you would be something of a job to mug, he's not going to attack you. If you are alert, confident, and moving quickly and purposefully along, you present a problem. Whenever possible, walk in a group, or at least with a friend; for that after-dark run to the convenience store, bring along your dog (and mind you, your dog doesn't need to be trained to attack; as long as your dog likes you he's going to stand by to repel boarders).

If you are strolling along with your nose in a book and your Walkman on, you might as well just drag your wallet on a string behind you and save everybody some trouble.

Choose well-lit, well-travelled routes. Vary your routine so that no one can say with certainty, "At 3:00 P.M. the little blonde will be walking through the parking lot behind the hospital." A mugger does not want witnesses or heroes, so stay where there are people for as much of your route as possible.

When you park your car, choose a well-lit place as close as possible to your destination. If possible, avoid parking next to trucks or vans that could block your view or conceal an attacker. You want to be able to see your car while you are still some distance away, and you want people to be able to see you if you should run into difficulty. When you come back to your car, have your keys already in your hand; while you are still some distance away *look underneath your car*. Be alert for any sign of movement. Someone could grab you by the ankles and pull you down while you are standing there fumbling with your keys. Quickly cast an eye over the adjacent vehicles; someone sitting idle in a parked car is a potential attacker or a potential source of aid—just be aware. Information is always valuable.

If there is someone hanging around near your car, especially if it is after dark or in a deserted place, do not worry about looking stupid. Turn around and go back to a lighted, populous location. If the person is still there when you check back after a few minutes or more, call a friend to come pick you up, or call a cab, or ask the kindly police officer to walk you to your car. It is much better to look like a goober than to get hurt. Two more brief car-related notes: Always have an extra $20 on you for cab fare or other emergency, and whenever your gas tank gets below half full, fill it back to the top. Running out of gas in unfamiliar territory is not smart.

Choice of clothes is another consideration. This is probably easier for me at middle-age than it is for you younger people, but loose clothing in which you can move easily is a safer thing to wear than, say, a tight skirt and high heels. This is not a sexism issue, so I don't want to hear any talk about how you should have a right to dress how you want without fear of sexual assault—of course you should. You shouldn't even need to be reading these notes, but in this sad and violent day, here you are. Dressing comfortably and practically is a matter of the mechanics of survival. You should be able to run, climb, punch, and kick in whatever you are wearing.

You're excused from this rule when you're in a chauffeured limo going to the Academy Awards. Then you'll be in brightly lit crowds, so you are probably okay with whatever silly thing you want to put on. But don't forget to wear your seat belt.

Finally, sometimes there are no good choices, and sometimes you get mugged anyway even if you make all the right choices. Nobody is completely mug-proof. I could get mugged on the way home from teaching a self-defense class. Perhaps a little ironic, but it wouldn't mean that any of this is bad information. The best you can do is try to improve your chances; sometimes you are just plain out of luck and there is nothing you can do about it.

In the worst case scenario, you get mugged, and you have to fight. I'll show you how to fight throughout this book, but the first thing you have to discover in yourself is the willingness to fight. Somewhere inside you there is a tiger pacing in a cage, and he's one pissed off bad boy. When the time comes that you must defend yourself, you have to find a way to open the door of the cage and let that tiger out.

You can't fight tentatively. You can't sock a guy in the nose and step back and see if maybe that was enough. You have to fight like an animal protecting its young.

The nature of the beast that is us means that it can be a terrific release to let that restless tiger loose, ready to ransack, pillage, and plunder. Don't be afraid when you get attacked, *be the tiger.*

LIZ'S TOP THREE SELF-DEFENSE DRILLS

1. Meditation
2. Jogging
3. Sit-ups

Meditation

Meditation clears the mind and enables you to focus your attention as necessary. Your brain is the most important item in your self-defense arsenal, and regular meditation keeps it toned and healthy. If you practice meditation daily, your peripheral awareness will increase. Your senses will become more acute. Your reaction times will improve. Here are some really basic meditation techniques.

Breathing Exercise 1

If you have ever spent time with a very young infant, you will be able to picture the kind of breathing I mean. When a baby inhales, its belly gets round and fat. On the exhalation the belly deflates. There isn't much rib movement, and the shoulders don't move at all. To practice a good way to breathe while meditating, lie on your back on the floor. Put one hand, palm down, on your stomach, and put the other hand on your chest. When you inhale, concentrate on pushing out your stomach to make the lower hand rise. Feel your ribs expanding laterally (if at all), and picture the air flowing into you like water. When you breathe out, feel your hand sink back down as though it were going to rest on your spine below your skin.

Breathe very long and slow. Try breathing in through your nose and out through your mouth. Imagine that the air you are breathing in is blue, and the air that you are breathing out is a hot and sticky red.

Sometimes I picture the baby in my head while I breathe. Sometimes I picture a fire about two inches below my navel, and every time the air flows over it, it glows brighter and hotter. Find a picture in your head that works for you. It doesn't always have to be the same picture.

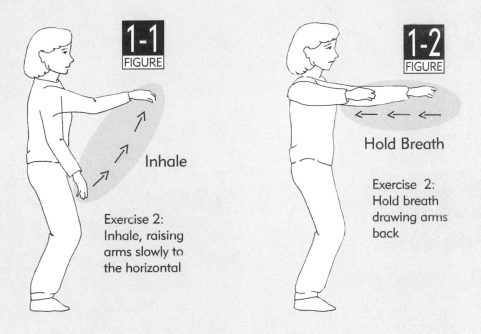

Exercise 2: Inhale, raising arms slowly to the horizontal

Inhale

Hold Breath

Exercise 2: Hold breath drawing arms back

Breathing Exercise 2

Standing up, place your feet parallel to each other just a little more than shoulder-width apart. Bend your knees slightly. In karate this is often called a horse stance.

Let your arms hang loose in front of you, palms toward you. As you inhale (through your nose, filling up your stomach), let your arms float gently upward as though the air you are breathing in were filling up a large balloon in front of you on which your arms are resting (Figure 1-1).

When your outstretched arms are at the height of your shoulders and parallel to the floor, pull your hands back toward you, as though they were caressing the top surface of the balloon. Hold your breath during this part as though that is what keeps your hands suspended (Figure 1-2). Then breathe out slowly, through your mouth, allowing your hands to sink back toward the earth as though they were resting on the deflating balloon in front of you (Figure 1-3).

Try counting in your head slowly as you do this. Breathe in for a slow count of three as your hands rise, hold for a slow count of three as they float toward you, and breathe out for a slow count of three as your hands fall back to their original position. Repeat this at least a

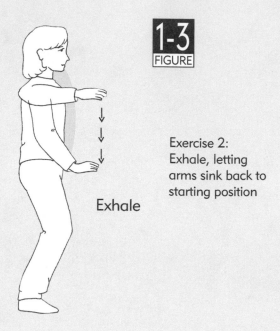

1-3 FIGURE

Exhale

Exercise 2:
Exhale, letting
arms sink back to
starting position

dozen times. If you get lightheaded you may be breathing a little too fast; work on slowing it down and keeping your breathing gentle and natural, not forced or strenuous. Keep it up for several minutes, breathing out long and slow, and your pace will self-regulate.

There are many "right" ways to meditate; this is just a place to start. Don't think you don't have time, either; even five or ten minutes a day is enough to make a difference. Plan to take a few extra minutes in private when you go into the bathroom for your morning shower. (I find the kids let you alone in the bathroom, at least for a little while.) When you go to get your laundry out of the machine and you find it's just begun the spin cycle, there's five more glorious minutes! And for those of you who work in an office, here are three words: big photo-copying jobs. I once did an entire tai chi form fourteen times, while making three hundred copies of a twenty-three-page exam.

It's not a big production to meditate; all you need are lungs and a brain.

Jogging (*or The Monty Python Technique*)

The first rule of self-defense is: If you can run away, do it. This is called the Monty Python defense after the scene in the Holy Grail where the rabbit attacks a band of knights who scramble to safety yelling "Run away! Run away!" I highly recommend this movie, by the way; consider its other invaluable contribution to the lexicon of fighting: "What'ch'a gonna do, bleed on me?"

The other name for the Monty Python tactic is Nike-do. There is nothing like a good speedy pair of legs to get you out of trouble. As Mr. Miyagi (of the *Karate Kid* movies) says, "Best defense is no be there." If you are on the next block by the time the fist lands, you won't get hit. Sprinting speed is probably more valuable than endurance.

Sit-ups

If the situation should arise where you can't avoid confrontation and you find you are actually forced to whack the mugger, you want it to be effective so you have to do it right. You want the mugger to feel as though the earth itself rose up to strike him down in all its awful majesty.

A hand strike actually begins from the heel of the foot. Picture, if you will, a ball of light that is the force generated when your heel pushes against the floor. In your mind's eye now see that ball of light travel up your leg, up from your hip to your shoulder, and along your arm to explode out of your fist as you make contact with whatever piece of the bad guy's anatomy you have chosen. Blam. The floor has just hit the bad guy. Your body was just the path it took.

During the course of your day, chances are your legs will get some use. You have to climb the occasional stair, walk to the cafeteria, whatever. Your arms, too, do some form of movement, even if they just keep your fingers poised above the keyboard. You have to put groceries in the car, chop the veggies for dinner.

Your stomach is another story. If you don't deliberately take some time to work with the muscles in your abdomen, they basically atrophy to a minimal level of functionality. Sitting up straight will use them to some extent but not nearly enough. When it comes to fighting, your stomach muscles transfer the power from your legs to your arms (note the path of travel of that imaginary ball of light). They enable you to pick your leg up swiftly to kick out somebody's kneecaps or send his nuts up to his throat (all you menfolk at home wincing yet?). Finally, they can absorb the force of a blow to your soft and tender midsection that might otherwise leave you gasping and helpless on your hands and knees.

Stomach muscles—don't leave home without them.

I would suggest doing sets of crunch-type sit-ups three times a week. For this kind of sit-up, you lie on your back with your feet flat on the floor and your knees bent. Naturally, if you haven't done sit-ups in a while (or a decade), you should start really slowly. Check out the following list and do one of each kind. Hook your toes under the edge of the couch when you start. This allows your thigh muscles to take up where your stomach muscles are falling down. Your goal is to be able to do twenty each of ten different kinds of sit-ups, as follows:

1. Clasp your hands behind your head, keeping your elbows extended out to the side like wings so that you are not using your arms to pull up on your head. Sit up only until your shoulders are four to six inches off the floor, and then go back down. Do twenty.
2. Cross your arms across your chest, and do twenty more.
3. Put your hands back behind your head, but now pick your feet up off the floor as though you were sitting on a chair that had been laid down on its back on the ground. Keeping your feet in this position, do twenty.
4. Put your feet straight up in the air, ankles crossed. Do ten, then cross your ankles the other way, and do ten more.
5. Lie on your back as though you were doing #1, above, but this time kick your feet up in the air, bring your knees back to the sides of your head, and bring your butt off the floor a few inches instead of your shoulders. Do twenty.
6. Place your right ankle on your left knee, and then bring your left elbow up to touch your right knee. Do twenty.
7. Put the left ankle on the right knee and use the right elbow. Do twenty.
8. Lie on your side, knees bent slightly. Place the forearm of the arm on which you are lying across your waist. Bend your other arm so that your elbow points to the sky and your fist is at your ear. Raise your shoulders up so that your elbow moves toward your hip. Do twenty.

9. Roll over and do the other side. Twenty.
10. Lie back on your back as for #1, but this time hold your arms up, one hand holding the wrist of the other, which has the fingers straight, together, and pointing at the ceiling. Do full sit-ups, making sure your hands travel straight up so that you end up with your elbows next to your ears like a diver going into a pool, and your hands reaching for the ceiling. Do ten, then change hands and do ten.

There, two hundred sit-ups. It takes less than ten minutes. It won't make you thin, but it will make you punch hard and kick fast. And, if you get socked in the gut, you won't puke. Always a plus.

THE ABCs OF STRIKING AND KICKING

Striking

Think of learning to fight as though you were learning to speak a foreign language. You can't expect to just start chatting colloquially. Think of it as a language like Greek, where even the letters are unfamiliar (that karate stuff is all Greek to me).

Throwing a good strike or kick is the alphabet of fighting. Let's start by examining the striking parts of your body.

First, make a fist. Close your fingers up tight, with your thumb on the outside to lock forefinger and middle finger down firmly. The striking surface of this fist is the top part of the first two knuckles (Figure 1-4). No matter how you hold this fist, either thumb down, thumb up, or thumb to the side, the striking surface remains the same.

There are other places you can hit with when your hand is clenched in a fist. You can hit with the flat back of your hand, or either the thumb or the pinky side.

It is important to remain relaxed and focused. Think of your fist as a rock and your arm as a rope that attaches the rock to your shoulder.

Try this exercise. Stand in your horse stance. Remember this? Feet just more than shoulder-width apart, knees bent. Allow your arms to hang limply at your sides. Pivot your body in one direction and then the other, allowing the arms to swing loosely in reaction to the pivoting (Figure 1-5). Your arms will start to feel very heavy and your hands may tingle. Do this for a while so you really get the right feeling. Let your hands swing freely

Striking
surface of
the fist

1-4
FIGURE

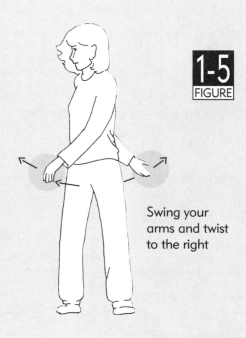

1-5
FIGURE

Swing your
arms and twist
to the right

and thump into your body as you change from one direction to the other (Figures 1-6 to 1-7).

Next, keeping your horse stance and keeping your arms flopping at your side, thrust your right hip forward so that your limp right arm flops forward, instead of coming around, the way it did in the first part of the exercise. Breathe out as you jerk your hip forward and your arm swings out. Do this first with one arm, then the other. Notice how when one arm swings forward, the other swings out behind you.

For part three of this exercise, being careful to keep that loose, fluid feel, use the thrust of the hip (push off with your heel, remember), add some impetus from your brain and your arm to the natural flow of the movement, and throw your fist, the rock, forward toward the target (the bad guy). At the same time pull back on the other elbow and bring your other fist up against your waist (Figure 1-8). Then throw the other fist out, bringing the first fist back, like a pushme-pullyou (Figure 1-9).

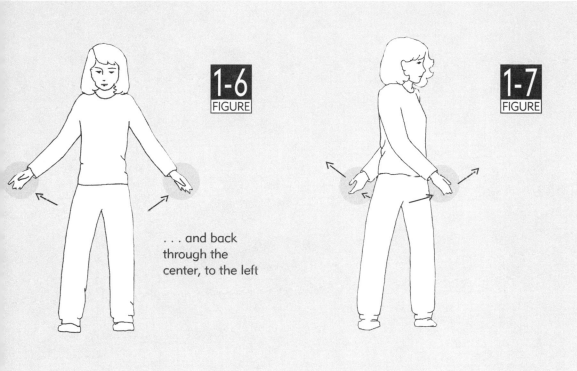

FIGURE 1-6

FIGURE 1-7

. . . and back
through the
center, to the left

Now instead of letting your arms hang limp between punches, keep them cocked at your sides, elbows bent, fists resting lightly, thumbs up, pulled against your waist. They should still hang loose from the shoulder joint. This brings your striking element, in this case your fist, closer to your center (that spot a couple inches below your belly button that you focus on when you do your meditation breathing). Your strongest strikes originate from close to your center and travel straight to the target. Remember to breathe out on each strike. Holding your breath will prevent you from striking with full power. Also, it is vitally important to keep your shoulders, hips, and heels all in the same plane throughout the strike, even at the fullest extension of your punch.

As soon as you feel yourself pushing out your punches with your arm muscles tense, go back to the exercise by flopping your arms around from side to side until you feel like Raggedy Ann again. Tension from the arm muscles creates resistance, which will mean that you are getting in your own way and slowing yourself down. Speed translates into power, so the faster a strike is, the better it will penetrate. (Imagine if you just tossed a bullet by hand as opposed to shooting it out of a gun.) Bruce Lee was not a big guy but he was unbelievably fast—he could get a punch going so quickly in the space of an inch that he could knock a big guy back several

The correct way to throw punches

The correct way to throw punches

feet. He was quite famous for this well-documented feat ("the one-inch punch"), and clearly it didn't work because of his overwhelming size because he was a wee fellow.

Your fist is not the only thing you can hit with. Consider your arm. Besides that handy (groan) fist out there at the end, you can try tucking your hand out of the way so that the ends of the forearm bones are the foremost protrusion. Voila, a new striking surface, less vulnerable than the small and delicate bones of the hand (Figure 1-10).

Better still, however, is the elbow, which can be used to smash laterally or drive forward, backward, up, or down. A self-defense situation is likely to be a close-in situation ("If you can run away, you should run!" Sound familiar?), so the elbow is often your weapon of choice. You can practice throwing an elbow to someone's head. Stand in your horse stance, fists at your side, and draw an arc outward and upward in the air with the point of your elbow that ends when your fist is at the opposite side of your face (Figures 1-11 through 1-13). If you are practicing hard and fast, it is possible to clip yourself in the ear or the jaw, so go slowly at first, please. (Can you say "voice of experience"?) Remember to push off the floor with your foot, breathe out, and stay relaxed as you practice.

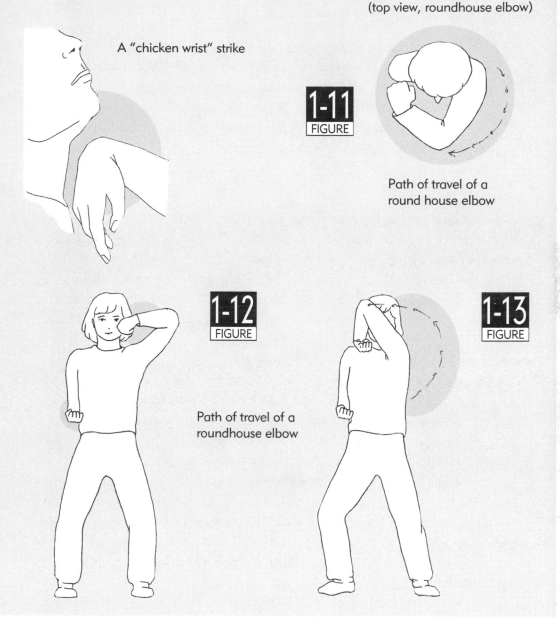

1-10 FIGURE

A "chicken wrist" strike

(top view, roundhouse elbow)

1-11 FIGURE

Path of travel of a round house elbow

1-12 FIGURE

Path of travel of a roundhouse elbow

1-13 FIGURE

Fun Practice Drills

1. Hang a ping-pong ball from a string and try to punch it CORRECTLY; breathe out, using speed instead of muscle.
2. Hang a piece of paper, ditto.
3. Have a friend hold a piece of paper from either side while you try to punch through it. You will quickly find that speed, not power, is your friend.

4. Wad a piece of paper into a ball and toss it in the air. Try to punch it *correctly* as it falls. Easy, right? Now make TWO wads of paper and toss them up simultaneously—punch each one before it falls. Now try THREE wads of paper. Do you sense a pattern? If you find you can punch four or more wads of paper before they hit the ground, you are very, very quick.

Kicking

Kicking is not just for those karate guys, but you should leave the kicks to the head to them. I know a high kick looks really cool but, unless you're very experienced, a kick is pretty easy to catch, and you can imagine how NOT fun it is to have the bad guy hanging on to your leg while you hop around on one foot like a dork. Remember, we don't care if we look cool, we just want to—lemme hear you, folks—GET HOME SAFELY. So don't give your attacker any help by providing something easy for him to grab.

For a good kick, you need to get your foot close to your center before your strike. Just the way a good punch comes from near your center and travels straight out to the target, a good kick has to start at the right place.

Start from your horse stance, remembering as always to keep your knees slightly bent. Pick up one foot and hold it up an inch or so away from the knee of the other leg (Figure 1-14). Now, wherever you point your knee is where your foot will kick. You want to snap a kick out quickly and pull it back just as quickly. From a forward-facing position, you can kick forward, sideways, or backward, but you always have to start by chambering the leg in this fashion for a really strong, pene-trating kick.

As there were different places on your hand to strike with, there are different places on your foot (Figure 1-15). Which piece of your foot you will use will depend on which direction you are striking. You NEVER want to kick with your toes. Toes are little and floppity and fragile; they break easily and hurt like fun when they do.

If you are kicking forward, you want to pull those toes back and let the ball of your foot hit the target.

If you are kicking sideways, you still have to pull the toes back and out of the way (Figure 1-16), and then turn the foot sideways so that the toes are aimed in a forward direction, making the heel the point of impact (Figure

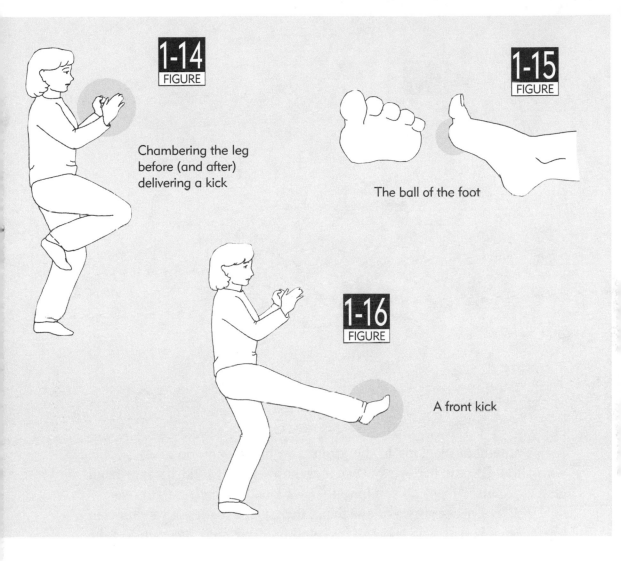

Chambering the leg
before (and after)
delivering a kick

The ball of the foot

A front kick

1-17). If you leave the toes pointing up toward the ceiling they will get in the way and lessen the impact of the thrusting heel. And hurt your toes.

If you are kicking backwards, keep the toes pointing down and thrust out the heel.

Good targets for any kicks are:

1. Stomping down on the instep.
2. Kicking the knee, either backwards, against the direction of the joint, or from the side. If you want to really damage the knee, aim just above it, not right on it or just below it.
3. The famous shot to the groin. You can use the top of your foot for this one, this time pointing the toes forward out of the way while you bring your instep smartly northward to the jewels.

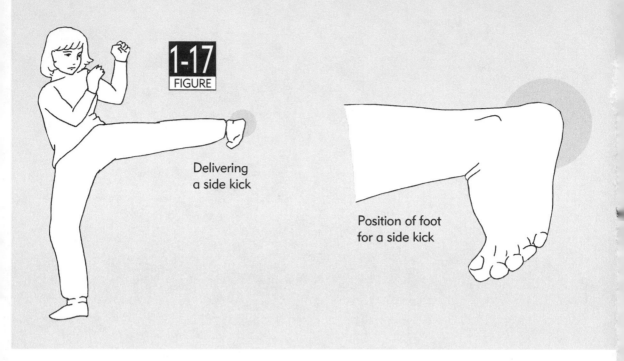

Delivering
a side kick

Position of foot
for a side kick

A note about kicking to the groin: I've heard way too many people who should know better say that they know they would be safe from attack because "really all you have to do is kick the 'nads—fight over."

Well, not necessarily. For one thing, there is the matter of varying pain tolerance. A person who is out of his mind on drugs may not even feel the pain until he wakes up the next morning; in the meantime, you have just succeeded in really pissing him off. Oh, goody.

Also, guys have had that thing dangling out there unprotected for their whole lives and they have developed pretty good instincts for deflecting any attacks that come its way. They like it in the fond and affectionate way that one likes a child or a pet. So it's really not your best choice of target—only go for the nuts if nothing else presents itself and you've got your attacker otherwise distracted.

Finally, a kick to the nuts, while not a pleasant thing, is not structurally incapacitating unless you break the pubic arch above, which takes one hell of a kick. Breaking the knee (which only takes about eight pounds of lateral pressure, according to some sources) will leave him lying on the floor unable to give chase, as will crushing a metatarsal or two.

When the mugger can't give chase, that's your cue. Don't wait for the cops, just GO. In this crazy day and age, the guy will sue you and win. From jail, even.

TARGETS

Now that you know *how* to hit and kick, it is time to discuss *where*.

Punching the bad guy in the big hard cranium with your fist, which is made up of bones about the size of doggie treats, is likely to be detrimental to your fist. Once again, your most important weapon is your brain, and when it comes to hitting, you'd better use it. Don't you hate that scene in the movie where the heroine thumps her pretty fists against the baddie's chest? How much effect does it have? Zip, zilch, nada.

I hate that scene too. I'm the one in the theater (you've probably heard me) who is saying "Head butt to the nose! Poke him in the eyes! Rip off his ears!" I assure you, if your hands are free you can make the bad guy drop you as long as you don't blow your chance and start slapping at his chest like a—gag—girl.

Let's start from the top and work downward (Figure 1-18). On the head, you can poke the eyes—this is not for the squeamish, okay? No delicate prodding; grab the sides of his head with your four fingers and drive your thumbs into the corners of his eyes nearest his nose. Think about popping those suckers out like a couple of peeled grapes. They're actually anchored in there by means of eye guts (a technical medical term), but you can make sure he is uncomfortable enough to let go of you and blinded enough not to give chase.

Ears are good—they are a convenient flap to grab hold of and twist (did your mean nanny ever do this to you?). You can also drill the knuckle of your first finger straight into the hollow leading to the drum. Try that gently on yourself, it hurts a fair bit. You can smack hard with your full palm against the ear, which forces air into it and in all likelihood will pop the eardrum.

There's a good spot at the back of the jaw that is easy to locate. Place your four fingers of each hand behind your partner's head. With your thumbs, find the hollow just below the ear and behind the jawbone. Push (gently please, on your partner, but with enthusiastic vigor on an attacker) in, up, and slightly back toward you, as though you wanted to drive your thumbs out the top center of the attacker's forehead.

A solid smack to the nose, either with a fist or a palm, will cause instant bleeding, solid pain, and fill the eyes with tears, which will impair vision for a few minutes. If you get a chance to punch it twice, that's even better.

I avoid punching the mouth—the bad guy's teeth could cut your hand severely, and AIDS notwithstanding, the human mouth is just a bacteria-fest.

The throat can be attacked in a number of ways. If you have enough distance to get a strong punch going, a punch to the throat can crush the attacker's windpipe. If you don't have enough space between the chin and shoulders to fit your whole fist, use the blade edge of your hand in the classic karate chop. If, for example, the bad guy is holding you close, perhaps trying to throttle you, put your first and second finger together (cross them slightly for more support) and dig them *in* and *down* right at the hollow of the throat where the collarbones meet. Be warned: this can be lethal if you do it with sufficient force. Try it gently on yourself to see how ugly it feels.

Also, if your attacker is a guy, as is statistically likely, you can use your fingers like pincers. Place your thumb on one side of the Adam's apple and your first two fingers on the other. Just grab onto it, dig your fingers *up* and *in*, and then pull smartly. You can make a woman uncomfortable with the up-and-in routine, but it's not as effective.

Let's move on to the area below the neck (Figure 1-19).

If you are at all ticklish, you will know that the armpits are loaded with bundles of nerve endings close to the surface of the skin. If you get a clear opening to punch somebody there, you are likely to deaden the entire arm for anywhere from minutes to hours. I don't want to suggest kicking this high because, as I mentioned before, high kicks are easy to catch if the kicker is not very experienced.

Remember putting two fingers together to dig at the throat? Starting at the lowermost point of the armpit, where the major muscle groups meet and form a V shape, there lies a stretch of sensitive spots that respond to having those prodding fingers or the forefinger knuckle drilled into them. Practice this one on your partner, but do stop the minute he starts yelling. If you go all the way down the sides for the length of the rib

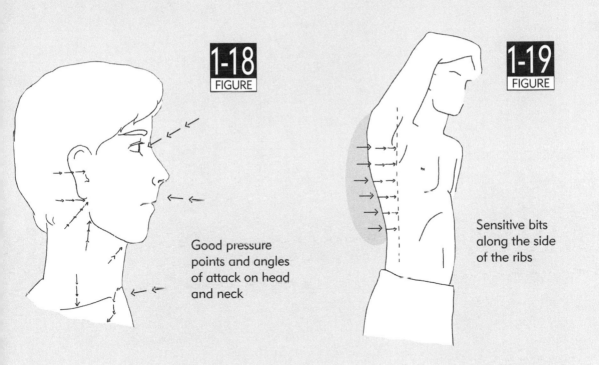

1-18 FIGURE

Good pressure points and angles of attack on head and neck

1-19 FIGURE

Sensitive bits along the side of the ribs

cage you find that you can get a strong reaction. This is not a fight-ender, but it is useful to get someone who is grabbing you to loosen up, allowing you to escape the hold and either run away or do something more finite to the bad guy.

The solar plexus, located beneath the breastbone, centered between the ribs and about three fingers above the bellybutton, is a prime location for a well-aimed elbow or knee. You will knock the wind out of your attacker with surprising ease. Do NOT do this to your workout partner, because sometimes he or she will even throw up.

Now let's look at the area below the waist. As you may remember from the previous section, don't count on kicks to the groin. However, if you can distract your attacker and create the opening, this can be a conversation-stopper.

Just south of the groin is the tender area of the inner thigh. A severe pinch, getting a good handful of flesh between your thumb and first two fingers (karate people call this one a "monkey bite") will loosen up an attacker who thinks he has your arms pinned down by your sides. Just reach down, back, and, using the Braille method, grab a meaty handful.

1-20 FIGURE

Kicking to the inner thigh

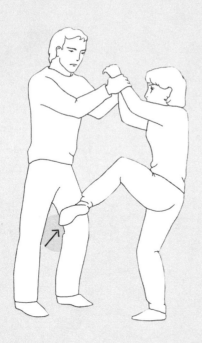

The inner thigh is also a good area to kick (Figure 1-20). The femoral artery runs along the inner thigh, and a really penetrating kick can cause significant internal bleeding. If the attacker has a strong hold on your hands or arms, pick up your knee and whip out your foot so that the top of your foot makes contact.

Knees are quite breakable. Kick above them, either to the back or to the side. (If you kick from behind, of course, they just buckle forward.) Just bring your foot to the joint and thrust through it, not at it—think of stamping your foot on the ground on the other side. Knees are a particularly good target in that they are structurally incapacitating. A guy with a busted knee is not going to chase you. Knee damage can be permanent, though, so if you must blow out someone's knee, don't stick around if you think you can get away with leaving the scene.

If you are really being held tightly enough so that all you can do is stamp your feet, go for the instep. The instep is vulnerable either to big sturdy boots or stiletto heels, leaving you with a number of fashion choices.

BLOCKING

Knowing how to recognize an incoming attack is essential. There is no good way to learn to do this except by practicing with a partner.

You should probably avoid looking at your attacker/partner's eyes. If you are actually engaged in a physical confrontation, it's better to focus on a point just below his neck, in the upper center of his chest. Aiming your eyes in this direction but maintaining a soft focus will allow you to detect any movement of his shoulders that will let you know that an attack is imminent.

There are two approaches to blocking. The first is that you strike hard at the thing that is attacking you. If someone throws a punch, your block is an attempt to break his arm. The second approach to blocking is to redirect the attack. I like this approach better because I want to set up the attacker so that I can strike hard at something more vulnerable than his arm—he can still chase me with a bruised or broken arm, can't he. So I would choose to redirect the arm and go in for the eyes or the knees or something more effective.

To practice redirecting, use your open hand with your fingers pointed upward, and have the heel of your hand make contact with your partner's arm as you try the following drills. Just re-aim the punch so that it pushes past you instead of hitting you. You'll know you're doing it right if your partner's forearms don't end up red and bruised. Think of using soft hands, like catching eggs—go with the punch and deflect it as you move back with it toward your body instead of banging it directly sideways on contact (Figure 1-21).

More Fun Practice Drills

To start Part 1, lean your back against a wall as you face your partner. Inch your feet out so that your back slides down the wall six inches or so, so that you are forced to remain stationary against the wall.

Have your partner stand with his or her toes against your toes, so that punches can actually reach you. Your partner should aim for the middle of your body so that if you don't block, you won't end up with a broken nose. Have your partner throw nice, easy, straight punches in a regular rhythm, first one arm and then the other. (You will find that the partner will tend to speed up right away, so it is often useful to put on some nice easy music with a regular beat and have the partner punch on the beat.)

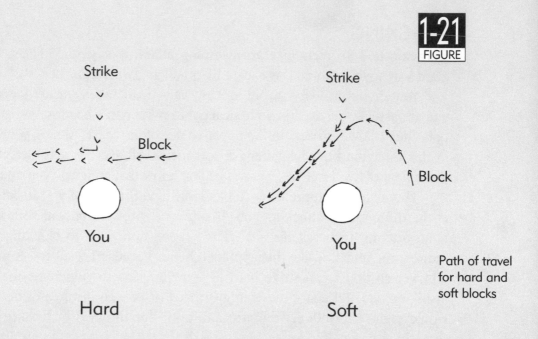

Strike

Block

You

Hard

Strike

Block

You

Soft

Path of travel
for hard and
soft blocks

I know, I know, I hear you saying "The mugger isn't going to throw nice easy punches on the beat, now, is he?" Of course not, but we are still learning the alphabet here. Stick with me, and I'll have you writing in no time.

Practice palming the block in different directions—redirect the punch out to your right, off to your left, over your head, down to the side.

Part 2 of this drill allows your partner to strike at either your head, your midsection, or your groin, but still in the same regular slow rhythm, using alternate hands to attack. He should attack at different heights in a random fashion so that you won't know which height of punch to expect.

Part 3 of this drill now allows the attacker to use whichever hand he pleases—three rights followed by a left, or any other combination—instead of alternating regularly.

Part 4 allows for variation in rhythm of attack. Here is where you turn the music off and let your attacker work randomly, attacking at any speed, any height, and with either hand. Your job is to just Zen out, soft focus on the center of the attacker's body, and keep those punches from making it to your body. You will get hit. It won't kill you.

By the way, as an aside, this is a useful thing to learn. The first time you get hit by another adult (as opposed to your cranky four-year-old who tells you that you are so mean), it can be a shocking experience. My God, you think, how dare they? If it is a solid hit, your eyes might tear up and then you are faced with worrying about whether you are going to cry and look like a baby, as well as wondering if you got—gulp—hurt or something. My early experiences with a sparring class were pretty rude. The first several times I got hit (because, frankly, I sucked), I would pretend my contact lens had come loose and I'd have to go to the bathroom to collect myself. Now when I get hit, which I often do (because it's all part of the exercise), it doesn't bother me at all. When I get up the next morning I find a fascinating collection of bruises, but except for the time that I broke my foot, I don't even remember how I got them. So you can get used to being hit, and after a while it really doesn't faze you. This is an important addition to your self-defense skills.

Lesson Two

HELLO, FLOOR

Lesson Two

LEARNING TO FALL

The counterintuitive portion of our program will now begin in earnest. You will hear me use the word *counterintuitive* frequently. Much of what you want to do (catch yourself as you fall to the floor, pull away from a grab, tense your muscles to punch hard) is exactly the opposite of what you ought to do. This is why I tell you that self-defense is not about being big and strong. It's about getting correct information in your brain so that you can be effective.

You may have fought against using muscle tension as you practiced your punches. Now, as you learn to fall, you will find that your instincts are even more likely to get in your way. Watch a baby who is learning to walk. Being up on two feet is a scary proposition, but when she teeters and plops back down onto her diapers, the baby rarely gets hurt because she is merely returning to terra cognita, the floor. However, you have spent years as a biped and the floor is several feet farther away from your brain than it is for the baby (although in the case of some guys it is only about half the distance that it is for the rest of us). You have probably fallen and hurt yourself more than once. Therefore when you lose your balance (or it is taken from you, in the case of a nasty push), you automatically stiffen up from fear of getting hurt.

Unfortunately, this is about the dumbest thing you can do, since the stiffer you are, the more likely you are to get injured. What you want to do when you see the floor coming is to say to yourself joyously, "Hello,

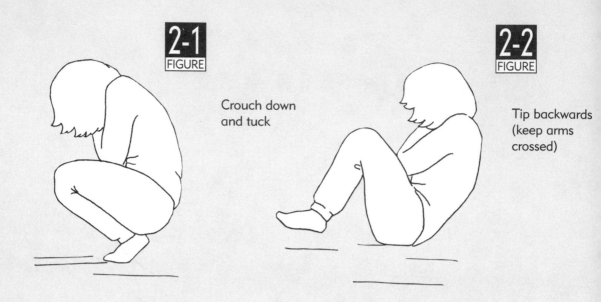

2-1 FIGURE

Crouch down
and tuck

2-2 FIGURE

Tip backwards
(keep arms
crossed)

floor!" and fling yourself onto it with gusto. You should be able to do this even without drinking many beers beforehand.

You can't change your instinctive reactions overnight. These reactions are like paths carved deeply into your brain by tiny road gangs. You need to take over from these gray-matter engineers and carve new paths. This takes time, patience, and many repetitions of the new actions so that they become your instinctive response. The first time you do the new thing, you are walking on virgin ground. Every time you do it again, whatever it is, you walk along that new path. After you've done the thing a thousand times, the new path will be the one your brain automatically chooses, and the old path will be all covered over with undergrowth. I hope you weren't going anywhere . . .

First, find a mat or a futon or something soft to flop onto. Squat down with your feet at the edge of the mat and your back facing it. (You can even practice on your bed if you are really nervous at first.) Cross your arms over your chest, tuck your chin down onto your breastbone (Figure 2-1), and make sure your teeth are closed—just a good habit to keep you from inadvertently biting your tongue. Curl your spine outward. Then gently allow yourself to tip backward, keeping your arms crossed and your head tucked (Figure 2-2), and feel how each of your vertebrae

Slapping out

touches against the surface in turn. When your shoulders are against the floor, allow your arms to open up and slap your palms down on the floor on either side of your butt (Figure 2-3). This is NOT to catch your weight; it is to stop the momentum of the backwards roll so you don't go on and roll ass over teakettle.

Do this many, many times until it feels very comfortable. Then try doing it on a regular floor with only a carpet. Next, ask your trusty partner to stand in front of you and give you a little push from the shoulders.

Gradually, as slapping out gets easier and more automatic, start from a progressively less crouched position. This could take days of determined practice; don't worry. It took you years to get this good at staying upright, didn't it? Your end goal is that when your partner gives you an aggressive shove while you are fully upright, you can collapse backward onto the floor and slap out without banging your head on the floor.

If you feel that you are stiffening up, you are probably expecting too much of yourself. Work within your own comfort zone; you'll get good at it with more practice. (My teacher often tells me that a thing "takes as long as it takes.") Just remember, every time you slap out, the new path in your head gets carved a little deeper. A lot of martial arts students report that they have taken unexpected falls from bicycles or down stairs and have automatically tucked and rolled or slapped out, and ended up

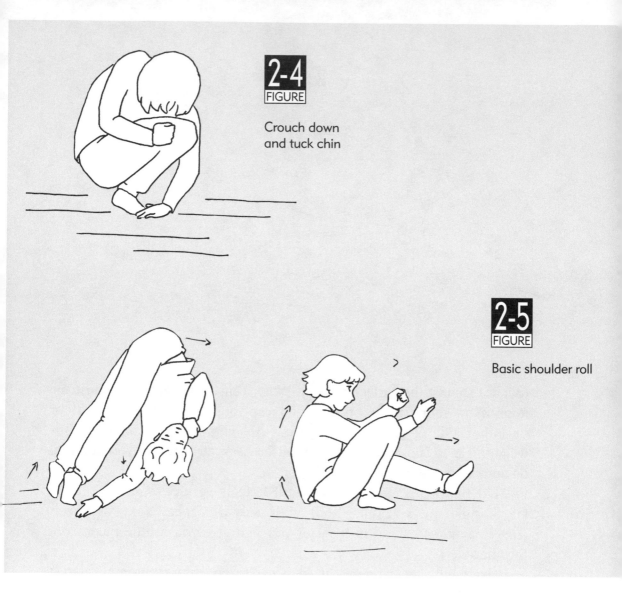

Crouch down
and tuck chin

Basic shoulder roll

without even a bit of damage. So this training will not be wasted even if you never do get mugged.

For a push from behind, you need to be able to roll forward. To practice this, squat down and face your soft surface (mattress, blankets, you name it). Tuck your chin and close your teeth, just like before. Now, with your head tucked as tight as it goes and canted off to one side slightly (Figure 2-4), place your shoulder blade down against the soft surface and push up with your legs so that your butt goes over your head and you end up rolling from the shoulder that you first put down over to the opposite hip (Figure 2-5). For those of you who did gymnastics in school (sucks boo to you), it's just a simple shoulder roll.

FIGURE 2-6

Keeping the attacker off with your feet

After you have mastered the shoulder roll from a squat, practice just the way you practiced slapping out, standing up a little straighter each time you roll.

When you get really good at it, try diving over an obstacle into a forward roll. Small children love helping with this part, as being in your way comes naturally to them. It's much easier than it sounds. As you push off into the dive, just remember to think cheerfully, "Hello, floor!"

Now you have learned what to do if you get pushed hard. You still might end up on the floor with the bad guy coming after you, but at least you won't be lying there stunned and helpless, having thwapped your head and skinned your hands and knees. With practice, you will end up on the floor unhurt, pissed off, and ready to rock and roll.

For the next drill, lie on the floor propped up on one elbow. Have a partner try to get close enough to put his or her hands around your throat. Your mission is to keep your legs—and particularly your feet—between you and your attacker (Figure 2-6). You can pivot on your hip, roll sideways, spin on your butt, whatever it takes, but make sure every time your partner thinks he can dive in on you, he collects a swift foot somewhere on the body. If you were really confronted by an attacker, you would kick—think now, where?—his knees, maybe, or up into his groin, or even into his solar plexus or face if he was bending down to grab. (That's the exception to the "high kick" rule: If his face is down where you can smash your foot into it, by all means, smash away. More on this when we get to the joint locks section.)

Remember, the mugger doesn't want someone who is a job. It is possible that when he finds that the push to the ground didn't render you helpless, he'll take off.

However, let's move on to the worst case scenario. He knocked you down and you couldn't keep him off, despite a determined effort to do so. You're on your back and he's straddling you, hands on your throat.

Point 1: If he can reach you, you can reach him. I won't relist all the targets, but you can figure them out. Ask your partner to simulate the situation and see what you can handily grab on to. If you can reach the ear and the chin, or, even better, the back of the head and the chin (depending on how far over he's bending), you can grab a fistful of hair (or an ear) in one hand and pull down. At the same time, you can get your palm under his chin and push up and away. Your aim is to control his head, although if you do this very quickly and forcefully, you will break his neck. You will spill him onto the back of his head onto the floor in any case.

You can also use your arm as a lever to pry him off you. Take your right arm and bring it over the outside of the attacker's left arm. Position the back of your right hand underneath his right arm, so that effectively your forearm forms a bar, or lever, between his two arms, over the first and under the second. Then take your left palm and place it under his right elbow (Figure 2-7). Tuck your right elbow into your body sharply while pushing up firmly on his right elbow, and once again, he should spill off onto the floor to your right side. Practice this with your partner.

If you find you are having trouble getting the attacker off of you using only your arms, push off the floor with your left foot, so that your left hip rises up just as you are tucking your right arm into your side. This will help to unseat the person on top of you. You can also try a monkey bite to the inner thigh, a punch to the groin, or digging your thumb into any spot you can reach as though you wanted to touch the bone underneath.

Your hands aren't your only weapons in this position. You can knee him in the back to break his balance and cause some damage, but don't just bring

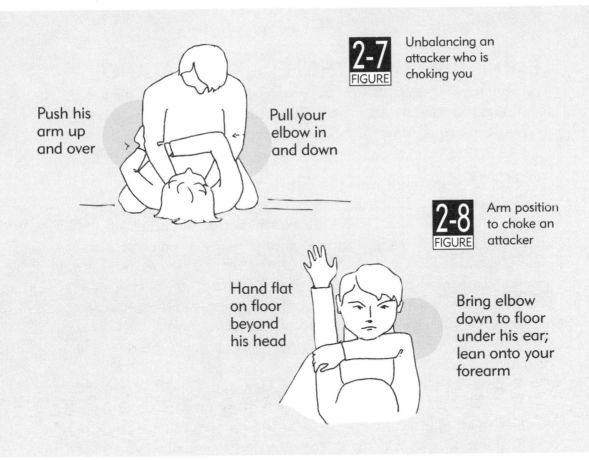

2-7 FIGURE Unbalancing an attacker who is choking you

Push his arm up and over

Pull your elbow in and down

2-8 FIGURE Arm position to choke an attacker

Hand flat on floor beyond his head

Bring elbow down to floor under his ear; lean onto your forearm

up one knee. Bring up your right knee and thump him, and then drive the right foot forward and pull up your left knee with everything your stomach muscles can offer. (The right foot acts for the knee like the returning elbow did for your hand strikes.) As soon as you feel his grip loosen, push down on one arm and palm up on the other, buck your hips, and knock him off.

Great, so now he's on the floor next to you. You can either roll away and run (Monty Python technique), or you can roll right with him and get on top of him (how do you like *them* apples, Mr. Mugger?). Immediately place your right forearm across his throat and put your left hand palm down on the floor at the side, slightly out in front of your attacker's head. Grab your left arm with your right hand for leverage (Figure 2-8). Then just lean your weight onto your right forearm and wait for his eyes to bug out. Push until he goes to sleep, although he may turn a delicate purple first. Warning! This is not as fail-safe as it sounds; do not forget that the best choice is always to run away as soon as you have created the opportunity to do so.

LEARNING TO BREAK THE ATTACKER'S BALANCE

There are two schools of thought on how to take the bad guy to the floor: the Motorcyclist and the Clothesline Theory, and the Lemmings Theory. There is also a combination of the two—a floor takedown.

The Motorcyclist and the Clothesline Theory

Basically, if you get a person's various body parts moving rapidly in enough different directions (two is usually sufficient), the end result is he goes nowhere but DOWN. Picture someone riding a motorcycle at a good clip who comes to a clothesline strung about four feet from the ground, going from one side of the road to the other. If the lower part of his body is moving forward at umpty miles per hour, and the upper part of his body is, for all intents and purposes, suddenly moving backwards (in relation to the lower parts) at umpty miles an hour, the rider will become road pizza.

To practice, stand facing your partner. Have your partner step in and punch toward your chest with his right hand. (If you miss the block, you don't get smashed in the nose.)

Step out on your left foot so that it is next to your partner's right foot. At the same time, redirect the punch with either hand so that it goes to either side of your body (Figure 2-9). It doesn't matter whether you are inside the punch or outside—try it both ways, using either hand to block. Just be sure to parry the punch and end up with your left foot outside your partner's right foot. Correct footwork is about 98 percent of a good takedown.

Now bring your right foot around the outside of your partner's right foot and step down behind your partner, so that now you are standing hip to hip and shoulder to shoulder. There should be no visible space between you (Figure 2-10).

Your right arm will now do duty as the clothesline while your right foot becomes the motorcycle. Keeping your right leg straight, swing it directly backwards so that it goes between your partner's legs and ends up out in front of your partner. As you can see, this gets your partner's right leg moving forward. At the same exact time that your leg clubs into the back of your partner's leg, your arm, which you are holding out like a pole extending to your right, comes sweeping across your partner's upper chest, knocking his upper body back and down (Figure 2-11).

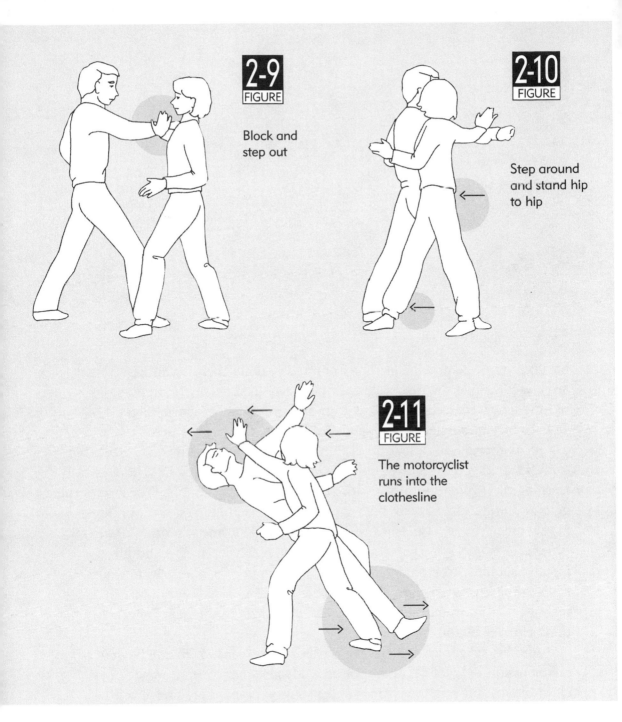

2-9 FIGURE

Block and step out

2-10 FIGURE

Step around and stand hip to hip

2-11 FIGURE

The motorcyclist runs into the clothesline

When you can get these two things to happen at precisely the same time, your partner will go onto the floor. Make sure he knows to slap out, as we discussed earlier.

It is good to work for a relaxed, fluid feel to your movements. If you are tense and choppy, the takedown will be less effective; tension will, as always, slow you down and make you get in your own way. If you are

2. Step around
behind on
right

Footwork for
takedown
(bird's-eye view)

1. Step out
on left

3. Bring right
foot back
quickly

having trouble getting the leg out from under, don't think about how you are going to smash into your partner's leg. Say to yourself, "I am going to put my foot *there*," choosing a spot out in front of your partner (Figure 2-12). Then, without further ado, put your foot on it.

Walk through the attack and setup for the takedown with your partner until you find you can move smoothly into the correct position. As you are learning, it is often useful to work technique in slow motion. When you get good at it at half-speed, then gradually increase until you are working in real time. You don't need to be good at it the first time you do it, or the fiftieth. Remember to keep your own weight over your feet, stand hip to hip and shoulder to shoulder, and relax. For practice purposes, swing your right arm across your partner at shoulder height to knock him over. In a real attack, you would punch the throat, palm heel to the nose, or something else debilitating in and of itself.

Another takedown you can try is called a leg reap, which can be done either inside or outside. It works on the same theory (motorcycle and clothesline), but this time you stand facing your partner, and when he steps in to punch you, you parry the punch to your outside as you step in. Jab out a little punch into his solar plexus to soften him up, and wrap your same-side (mirror image) leg around his forward leg (Figure 2-13). For example, if your partner steps in on his right, you wrap it with your left. Then you kick backwards with the wrapping leg while you strike to the upper body (Figure 2-14).

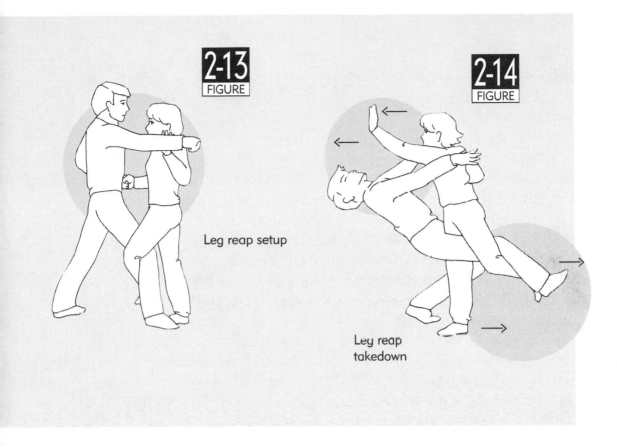

Leg reap setup

Leg reap
takedown

Once again, as far as the "clothesline" part of the exercise goes, for practice purposes you put your palm against your partner's chest and push. If it were a real bad guy, you would strike the same targets as in the first takedown instead (throat, nose, eyes), in an attempt not only to knock the bad guy over but also to do damage. But this will use up partners quickly, so we just thump them on the chest. A good workout partner is nothing to use up lightly.

Partner Consideration Lecture

At this time, I must briefly digress. When you are working cooperatively with a partner, you are doing your best to *simulate* an attack scenario. While you are being considerate of your partner by not *actually* killing him, he must also be considerate of you. It wouldn't hurt to take a few minutes to go over this section together.

Lack of partner consideration comes in two forms. The first way for him to be inconsiderate is the obvious: He refuses to let anything work on him, he stands stiff like a board, and he fights against the takedowns. All this will do is force you to be too rough so that the technique will come out right. For example, if a technique is set up with an elbow to the face, he should allow his weight to rock back onto his heels *even though you do not actually smash his nose in*. This will substantially change the way the subsequent moves flow together to form the technique. If the setup involves a knee to the solar plexus, he should allow himself to bend forward at the waist even though he has not just had the wind knocked out of him. Got it?

The other way for your partner to be uncooperative is to be too cooperative. Before his balance is even remotely broken he hurls himself to the floor with a resounding crash. The people who are likely to do this are the people who are not yet confident of their slap-out skills; they drop to the floor before they are thrown there because they prefer to go down under their own steam and therefore have more control over the rate of descent. He may not even realize he is doing this right away, but if it becomes obvious to both of you (and eventually it will) that this is his style, he should work on being a little less easy and spend more time privately working on his slap-outs.

If you feel that your partner is being too cooperative, you can suggest that he try to be a little tougher, but please understand that it is impossible for someone to just stop being afraid. Go gentler for a while, and if your partner is still slithering to the floor at the slightest provocation, try working occasionally with a different partner so that you have a chance to get a feel for making the technique work properly.

If you find that your partner is being too uncooperative, up the contact level enough to make the technique work anyway. When your partner is tired of minor bruises you will have an easier time.

The Lemmings Theory

Lemmings are cute little furry creatures that are not famous for being smart. What they know how to do, according to legend, is follow the guy in front. The problem is that, when they come to some potentially lethal obstacle such as a cliff or a river, the guys in front may want to stop but the teeming masses that follow continue to, well, follow. This forces the guys in front over the edge, or into the river. Then the guys behind say, "Hey, well, we've got to follow the guy in front," so over they go. The guys behind them say, "Gotta follow!" and over they go, and so on, until the whole not-very-bright horde has self-destructed. I've never actually seen lemmings do this, so it may all be a myth, but the image is useful for the other workable theory on breaking the attacker's balance.

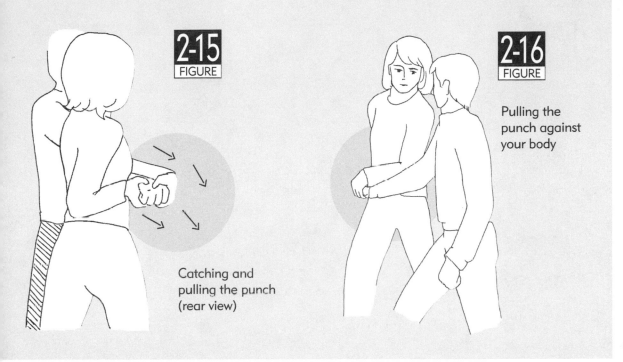

2-15 FIGURE

Catching and pulling the punch (rear view)

2-16 FIGURE

Pulling the punch against your body

The Lemmings Theory is this: Where one part of the body goes, the rest of the body has to follow. As these takedowns generally employ a modicum of leverage, that will leave us in a good place to pick up the thread during the next lesson, on joint locks.

Have your attacker step toward you and throw a punch. For the purpose of descriptive clarity, make it a right-handed punch (also the most statistically likely).

Step outside the punch on your left foot and turn your body so that the punch goes past you to your right. As the punch is passing you, come down on top of it with both your hands, and seize the punching hand by the meaty bits at the ball of the thumb and the opposite edge of the hand. Come over the top of the punch with your left hand and under with your right so that you are pulling the punch against your right side with your hands (Figure 2-15).

Now, as though you are driving a race car with a small steering wheel, keeping your elbows tucked against your sides, flip the punching hand over and pull it sharply across to your left side (Figure 2-16) as you step back onto your left foot (Figure 2-17). Your attacker's body will make a lovely midair arc if you do this smoothly and quickly.

All you did was catch the punch, swing it around, and twist it upside down, but suddenly there is the entire attacker, sprawled out and stunned. Hand flipped, bad guy flipped. Now you RUN.

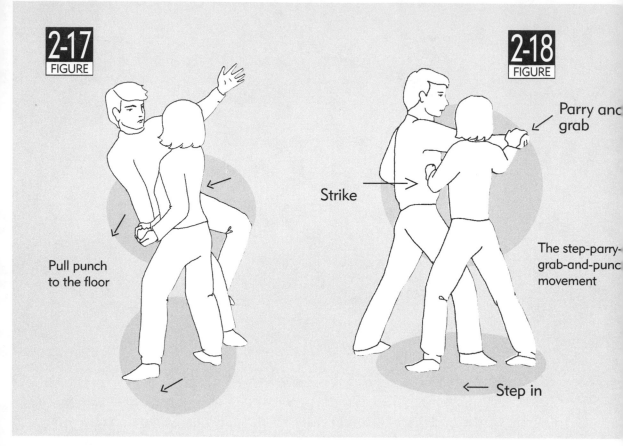

2-17 FIGURE

2-18 FIGURE

Pull punch to the floor

Strike

Parry and grab

The step-parry-grab-and-punch movement

Step in

If, after you step back, you kneel and put his hand firmly on the floor as the bad guy is flipping, he will land with a fairly resounding crash. Remember that when you are fighting bare-handed, the floor is always one of your potential weapons.

To try another setup for a lemmings takedown, have your partner step toward you and punch, as before. Again, step out on your left foot. This time put your right hand up to parry the punch off to your right. As your right hand follows along the arm and the path of the punch, close it over the back of the punching hand. Practice just this much for a while so you step in, parry, and grab in a smooth motion. You will find that your left hand is in a good position to strike your partner's floating ribs at the same time, if you have enough space in your brain left to add that refinement (Figure 2-18).

Once the step-parry-grab part is fluid, bring your left hand up under the punch as you turn the arm over with your right hand, which is still placed over the top of the punch. You will find that the easiest handle for this is the ball of the attacker's thumb, which has your four fingers wrapped around it from above (Figure 2-19). Now, raise the punching

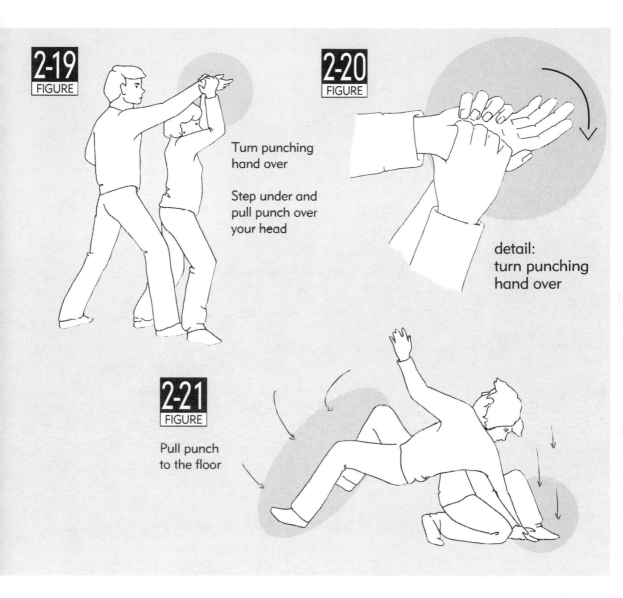

2-19 FIGURE

Turn punching hand over

Step under and pull punch over your head

2-20 FIGURE

detail: turn punching hand over

2-21 FIGURE

Pull punch to the floor

arm up and step under it with your left foot, which brings your back to your attacker's front while his arm is over your head *with the palm facing up*, and your hands are clamped onto the sides of his hand. Your right hand has the ball of his thumb, and your left hand has the blade edge of his hand, from pinky to wrist (Figure 2-20).

Now, kneel down and swiftly pull the punching hand straight down to the floor in front of you (Figure 2-21). Do not loosen your grip on the hand or allow it to roll between your fingers.

You can take other body parts and put them on the floor following this same theory. For example, let's say the attacker comes at you and you spring at him (counterintuitive, remember?). You grab his right shoulder with both your hands and drive your right knee up into his solar plexus (Figure 2-22).

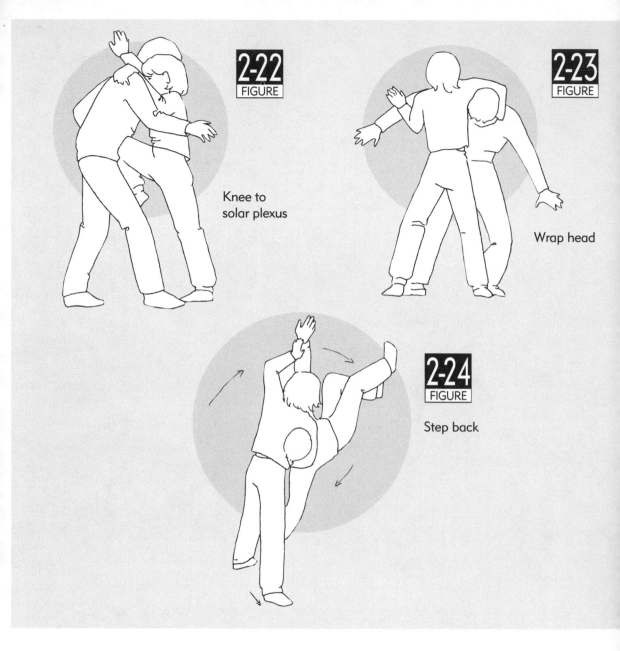

Knee to
solar plexus

Wrap head

Step back

This *will* bend him over, no kidding. As he doubles over, whooping, take your
right arm and wrap it around his neck so that you are holding his head
clamped to your right side (Figure 2-23).

Step back on your right foot and push up from under his right
shoulder or upper arm with your left hand as you pull down on his
head. Head flips, body follows (Figure 2-24). Be careful as you
practice! Necks are more fragile than you would believe, and pre-
sumably you like this person who is letting you learn with his body.

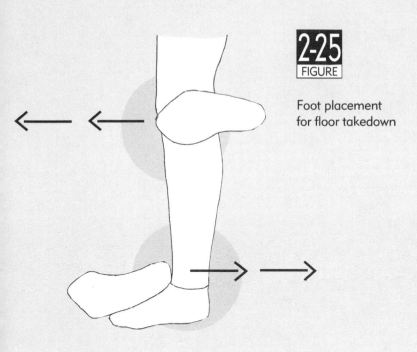

2-25 FIGURE

Foot placement
for floor takedown

Please allow the head and neck to slide around in your grasp, and let go completely as you step back. If you hold on too tightly and add just that extra bit of torque with your hip—well, save it for the bad guy. As it is, your partner should end up rolling along the floor, away from you.

Floor Takedown

There is one more tricky little takedown that might conceivably fit in either category. See what you think.

Lie on the floor on one side. (Imagine the bad guy knocked you down—it's unlikely that you would drop to the floor when faced with an attacker.) Hook your upper foot around the back of your partner's knee. Now take your lower foot and rest your heel in front of your partner's ankle (Figure 2-25).

Scissor your feet sharply. This will collapse the leg and bring the knee to the floor. So, the knee hits the floor and the body follows (lemmings), but the foot went one way and the knee went the other (motorcycle and clothesline). One of life's little conundrums.

Lesson Three

YEOWCH!

Lesson Three

APPLYING JOINT LOCKS

Practicing joint locks with a partner is the most uncomfortable lesson you will have in this series. Joint locks work on the theory of pain compliance. If you can make someone sufficiently uncomfortable, you can control him or her. Ex-spouses and/or ex-boyfriends make wonderful cannon fodder for practice. The children are likely to complain—ungrateful wretches. And after all you've done for them.

To understand viscerally (as opposed to merely intellectually) how a lock works and how it can be used to immobilize an attacker, you will have to allow your partner to really lock the joint in question, sometimes even to the point where you are taken to the floor. Don't just wince at the first sign of pain and say, "Ooh, ooh, I get it, that's enough." Pain will not kill you, and even though you may hurt enough to make you mutter evil words, you will not feel any ill effects when you get up tomorrow. Well, certainly not after a day or so. Your fingers might be a bit stiff for a day. Even so, let your partner apply the lock just about to the point where sweat is popping out and you feel a bit queasy, and then you will understand why it is that you can get the bad guy sprawled face down on the floor simply by grabbing a couple of his fingers and applying pressure.

Karate people talk about "tapping out" in the context of communicating with the partner. When a lock or submission hold is applied and becomes so uncomfortable that you would like it to stop unless someone is willing to shoot you to put you out of your misery, you slap your own thigh or the nearest surface (often the floor) two or three times in rapid succession. If the partner is a bully and doesn't let go, then you have my permission to slap the partner. And remember, you also get to do the technique to your partner, and what goes around comes around.

We will use most of our time discussing finger, wrist, and elbow locks, and touch briefly on locking the shoulder and immobilizing the head. The sweet thing about locking the smaller joints is that it pits your strength against one very small part of the other person's body. You do not have to be massive to make somebody else remarkably uncomfortable, as you have already learned in the "targets" section of this book.

Joint locks all work on the principle of asking a part of the body to bend in a way it was not intended to bend. To apply them you have to move quickly because they are not hard to escape until they are fully applied. Once you are cranking on a good lock, your partner should be too busy thinking, "Yeowch! Cut it out!" to get out of it.

Like everything to do with the structure and wiring of Homo sapiens, however, there will be myriad small differences mixed into the overall design plan. One person's pass-out-with-pain level will be another person's mild discomfort. Empirical data shows that women have more flexible joints and a higher pain tolerance than men, so if you can get your female partner on the floor wishing devoutly for your immediate demise, you can really wreak havoc with most men.

FINGER LOCKS

Picture the fingers as four pencils attached down at your wrist. If you grab one or more of these pencils firmly and bend it backwards, it will bend only so far before it breaks. If you apply pressure in two spots (pushing forward on the lowest joint and backwards on the tip of the finger), it will break that much more quickly since you are increasing your leverage (Figure 3-1).

Don't ever forget, though, that the bad guy can still chase you with a broken finger. For control, you want to get to the point just before the joint gives out and stay there. Have your partner reach out toward you as though he were about to snatch up a handful of your lapels. Reach your hand out to your partner's in the classic high-five response so that your palms meet midway between you. Curl your fingers around at least three if

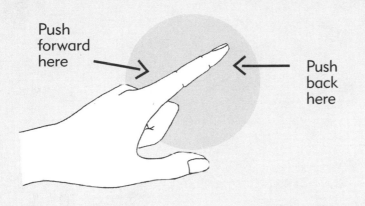

Push forward here

Push back here

Leverage spots on finger

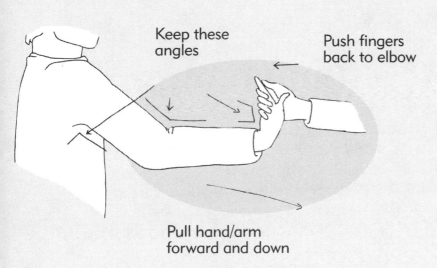

Keep these angles

Push fingers back to elbow

Angles of force

Pull hand/arm forward and down

not all four of your partner's fingers and press the fingers back toward the crook of the elbow while pulling out and down on the arm (Figure 3-2). You do not want to allow your partner to retract the arm because that will relieve the pressure on the fingers.

Keep pulling back and down, stepping back with your body and kneeling down onto the floor until you have your partner sprawled face down on the floor while you are maintaining constant pressure on his

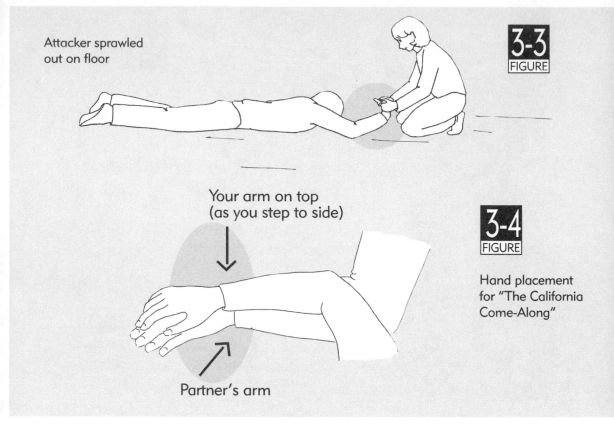

Attacker sprawled out on floor

3-3 FIGURE

Your arm on top (as you step to side)

3-4 FIGURE

Hand placement for "The California Come-Along"

Partner's arm

fingertips toward the crook of his elbow (Figure 3-3). You want the arm extended fully out in front. As soon as you have got your partner to the floor, lay off and let him up. He gets to do it to you next.

Try this on a few different partners so you will see how different people bend differently. Make sure with all your joint locks that you use your feet to keep you out of punching range. As you are only controlling a small piece of the other person, you must never forget that they have a free arm to hit with, if you are anywhere within reach.

I was taught that the next finger lock is called "The California Come-Along"; supposedly the California police use this technique to subdue miscreants. I have no idea if this is true, but it is a nasty little finger lock. (Of course, I mean "nasty" in the most admiring way!)

As the partner reaches in, you step to the side. (If the attacker is reaching with the right arm, you step to the attacker's right side.) Bring your arm down over the top of your partner's arm so that the palm of your hand is lying on top of his hand, with both sets of fingers pointing in the same direction (Figure 3-4). You will see that this means you and your partner are facing the same direction, also.

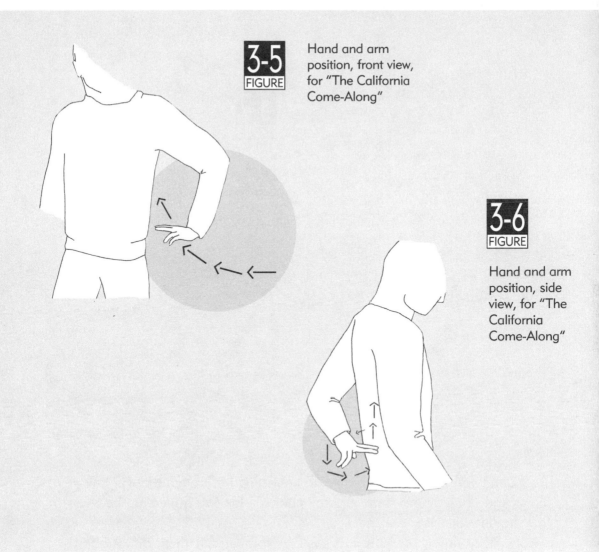

3-5 FIGURE Hand and arm position, front view, for "The California Come-Along"

3-6 FIGURE Hand and arm position, side view, for "The California Come-Along"

Close your fingers around the index and middle finger of your partner's hand. Bend them back to the crook of the elbow, and as you are bending, turn them in to point toward the partner's ribs as you force the arm back behind the partner (Figure 3-5). (This is the "break the pencil" theory again. Isn't it comforting when things are consistent?)

Still maintaining the pressure on the fingers, pull the hand out behind the partner's back until the partner is forced up onto tippy-toes (Figure 3-6). Then in a quick motion bring the hand in and sharply up between the shoulder blades, which should get the partner not only on the balls of his feet but also arched over backwards (Figure 3-7)—and probably yelling.

Hand comes
back and up
between the
shoulder blades

Can't you just picture an irate cop reaching in through the window of a car and bringing out some mouthy punk via his two fingers up between his shoulder blades?

A nice thing about joint locks is that you can use them on an offensive drunk without having to inflict the kind of structural damage you would do to a mugger in a dark alley. However, they can be used to set up the mugger so that you can do really severe structural damage. For example, when you have your partner at the last part of the California Come-Along, he is arched backwards with the upper chest and throat exposed. If you drop the heel of your palm with great force onto the sternum, you can actually kill the person but it would have to be an *extremely* forceful strike. Another target would be the exposed throat, but you already knew that. Remember, you only want to do what you have to do so that you can run away.

The better you get at joint locks, the wider your range of choices and the more time you have to do a carefully considered and effective strike.

There are many more beautifully vicious finger locks. Whole books have been written and courses taught on the subject. For our purposes

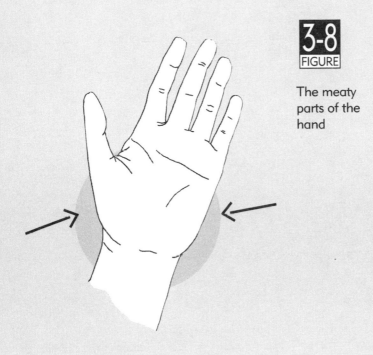

The meaty
parts of the
hand

and with our time limit, all you need to grasp is the principle of breaking the pencil. It will take some practice to get smooth and quick, and, unfortunately, it is hard to find partners who will let you practice on them. Keep trying!

WRIST LOCKS

You have already done an elementary wrist lock in the "lemmings takedown" section. To make a lemmings takedown work well, the part of the body that you place on the floor should be locked to ensure that the rest of the body will follow with alacrity.

The wrist can be locked out by taking hold of the meaty parts of the hand (Figure 3-8) and twisting them in either direction. You will find that twisting one way will bend the partner forward, and twisting the other way will bring the partner backwards.

A wrist lock can be applied with one or both hands. To make it work one-handed, you have to put your thumb on the back of the hand while your fingers wrap around and grasp either meaty part, depending on

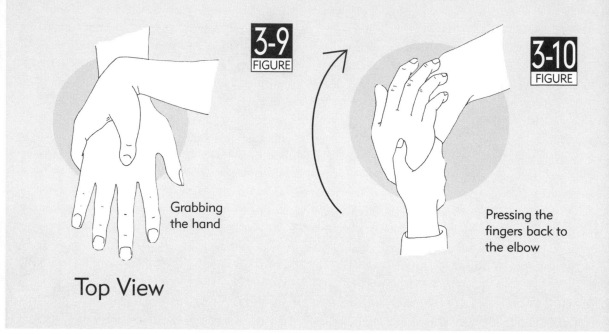

3-9 FIGURE

3-10 FIGURE

Grabbing
the hand

Pressing the
fingers back to
the elbow

Top View

which is closest. The thumb will give you sufficient leverage to turn the wrist and bend the partner.

Practice bending your partner both ways with the wrist lock. Have your partner put out an obliging hand and reach down on top of it so that your thumb is against the back and your fingers wrap around the meaty part at the blade edge of the hand (Figure 3-9). If your partner reaches out his right hand, you respond with your right hand.

You will note that this has your own elbow up and out in front of you. Tuck your elbow in to your side and push with your thumb as you turn your own hand over. This turns your partner's hand upside down and forces him to bend over forward. Keep the hands all close to you, so that your partner's arm is extended outward and your partner is easy to further off-balance with a (gentle!) tug on the hand as you twist. Make sure that you keep pressing the fingers back toward the elbow (Figure 3-10).

Whenever possible, when doing a technique, keep your shoulders over your hips, your back upright, and your knees bent so that you are stable and your center of gravity is low. You may find unconsciously that you are being considerate of your partner and leaning off balance so as not to disturb his center of gravity. Well, don't.

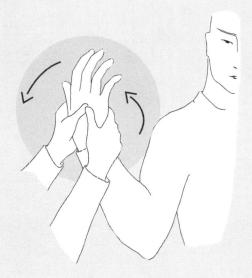

Bringing the
locked wrist up
to the shoulder

By now you have doubtless noticed that each joint lock uses footwork on your part. It is important to keep your body in the correct position with respect to your partner so that the joint is fully and easily kept in the locked position. Every time your partner adjusts his feet in an attempt to alleviate pressure, you must also adjust. A joint lock is not just a matter of simply keeping your hands in the right place. It is a matter of your whole body being positioned correctly. Your own balance must be maintained, your center of gravity must be low, and you must be standing in such a way with respect to your partner that you arc not vulnerable to counterattack. Try to be conscious of your feet as you practice. If they are too stationary, you are not doing the techniques as well as you might.

Now have your obliging partner stick out his right hand. This time, make the same grab as before with your left hand, so that your thumb is against the back of the hand and your fingers wrap around the ball of the thumb. As you bend the hand this time you will see that your partner leans over backwards to try to alleviate the pressure. If you also bring the hand up as though you wanted to put it behind the shoulder blade, while maintaining the pressure of the twisting motion, your partner will be brought to the floor virtually effortlessly (Figure 3-11).

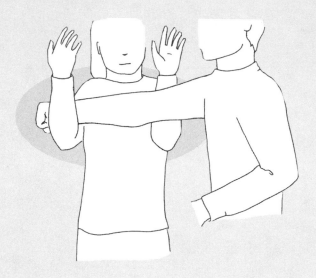

Trapping the
punch between
your forearms

ELBOW LOCKS

To work against a larger joint such as the elbow, you will find it is more
effective to use your forearms to trap, bend, and control than it is to use
your hands and fingers. This is logical, if you think about it. You need larger
weapons to deal with a larger attacker (or a larger piece of your attacker).

It is possible to lock out the elbow when it is straight by applying
pressure directly against its natural hinging motion. It is also possible to
lock out the elbow by applying pressure sideways against the joint. The
first way will result in bending the person forward; the second way will flip
the person backwards.

Have your partner throw a straight punch (or just stick out that
obliging sacrificial arm). For the sake of clarity of description, let's pick the
right one, as usual. Step in on your left foot, turning your body to the right
so that the punch slips past you. By now, you've done this before. Bring
your right arm up, hooking under the punching arm and pulling it into the
crook of your elbow. Bring your left arm forward against the attacking arm
so that your forearm makes contact just above the elbow and the punching
arm becomes trapped between your two forearms (Figure 3-12).

If you roll your left forearm up and over the partner's arm and then
push down while pulling up with the piece of it that is caught in the crook
of your elbow, you will force the punching arm's elbow to lock out straight
and the partner will bend forward (Figure 3-13). If you keep applying
pressure as you kneel and force the arm to the floor, you have an example

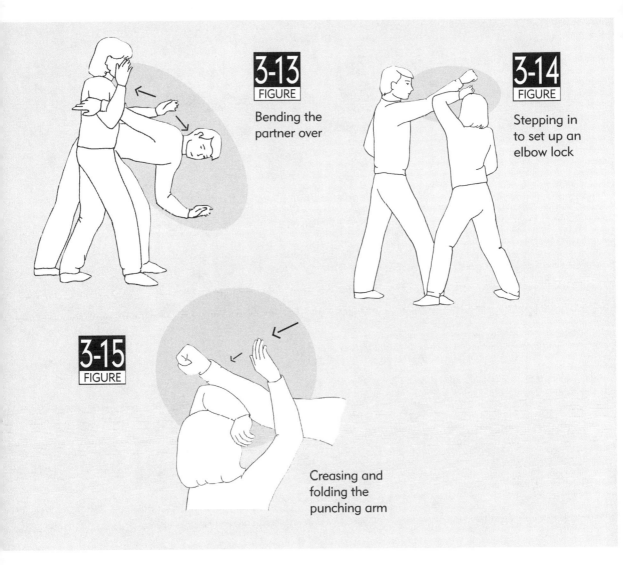

FIGURE 3-13
Bending the partner over

FIGURE 3-14
Stepping in to set up an elbow lock

FIGURE 3-15
Creasing and folding the punching arm

of yet another lemmings takedown; your partner will end up face down on the floor.

To work the lock in the other direction, have your partner throw a punch. (Note that this works even better against an attack that is coming down from above, as when someone comes at you with a stick or a bat of some sort. We'll look at this in Lesson 5.) Step in on your left foot and bring your left forearm up from beneath the punching arm, catching it about at the elbow or just below, and pushing upward (Figure 3-14).

Reach over the punching arm with your right arm and come down sharply across the crease of the elbow, which, as you are continuously applying upward pressure with your left arm, will cause the punching arm to fold in over your right arm (Figure 3-15).

Grasp your left forearm with your right arm, forming a triangle-shaped trap with the partner's arm through the middle, bent at the elbow

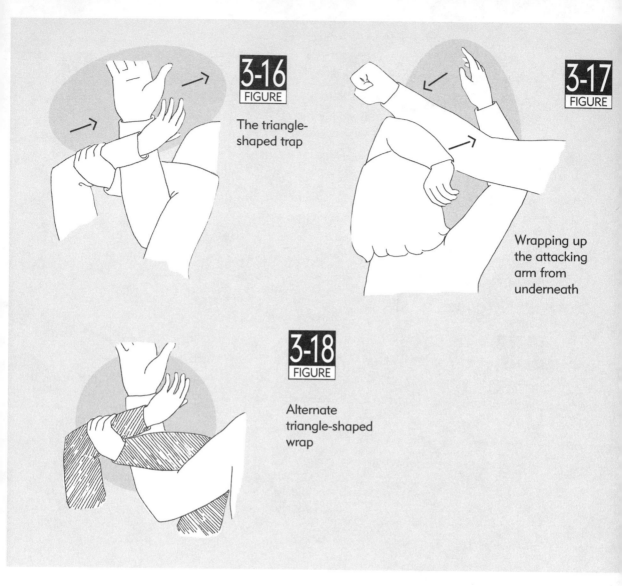

3-16 FIGURE

The triangle-shaped trap

3-17 FIGURE

Wrapping up the attacking arm from underneath

3-18 FIGURE

Alternate triangle-shaped wrap

and hand back to the shoulder (Figure 3-16). Walk forward, which will place your partner neatly down onto his back on the floor. You have enough control of the punching arm that you can do this gently (for your workout partner) or ugly (for the nasty mugger whose head you should whap onto the concrete sidewalk).

It is also possible to create the lock by reaching from underneath with your right arm after the block. In this case, you will snake your right arm up at the crook of your partner's elbow, forcing his arm to bend so that the hand moves in toward his shoulder (Figure 3-17). Bend his arm by pushing with your left forearm and pulling in toward you with your right forearm (Figure 3-18). At the same time, clasp your right hand around your own left wrist

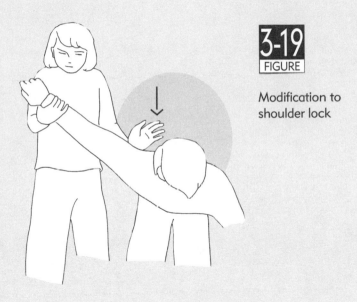

3-19 FIGURE

Modification to
shoulder lock

(Figure 3-18). I know this is starting to sound complicated, but look at the pictures. It's perfectly clear when you are doing it.

Now as your partner's wrist and/or forearm, with the combined weight of your two hands pressing on it, comes back to his shoulder, continue to press back and down on the forearm. Kaboomie. The partner once again is on his butt on the floor.

SHOULDER LOCKS

A quick word here on shoulder locks. With minor modification, the initial lock as described at the beginning of the elbow lock section becomes a shoulder lock. (Trap punch between forearms, bend bad guy over . . . if this doesn't sound familiar go make a cup of coffee and reread from the beginning of the chapter.)

When the pressure is applied to the elbow of the attacking arm while the attacker's wrist is trapped in the crook of your arm, the pain is generated in the elbow joint. Ergo, elbow lock.

To apply pressure to the shoulder, slide your left hand (in this case) up to the joint. Press the blade of the hand over and down into the crease of the joint, shifting your right hand to press directly up against the

3-20 FIGURE

Wrapping the neck

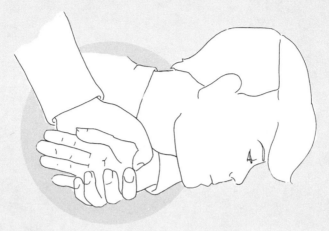

attacker's wrist (Figure 3-19). This causes the pain to be generated from the shoulder joint—ergo, shoulder lock.

HEAD LOCKS

A head lock isn't really a lock of the head proper, but there are interesting and useful things you can do to the neck when you have the head wrapped and immobilized.

Remember the technique from Lesson 2, where you drilled your knee into your attacker, bent him over, and then wrapped your arm around his neck? (Of course you do, and you've been practicing it faithfully all week.) You start with your partner facing you, and with your right arm, you reach up and around the left side of his head, pulling it down against your right-side ribs. (In Lesson 2, you softened him up with that knee to the solars, and then you stepped back and threw your partner onto the floor WITHOUT BREAKING HIS NECK.)

This time, instead of stepping and throwing (and possibly neck breaking), we'll try the following. As you wrap your right arm over your partner's head, bring it around so the hairy side of your forearm and the back of your hand lie flat against your partner's upper chest. You will see that the thumb side of your hand is directly against your partner's neck (Figure 3-20).

Take your left hand and reach down and close it around the meaty part of your right hand. Now (gently, please, unless you have an expendable partner) tighten the muscles in your right arm and pull up on your right hand with your left. This presses the thumb side of your hand up and into your partner's neck while your biceps muscle is pushing the head down, effectively doubling the pressure on the neck.

Do please stop *before* your partner passes out. I'm not kidding.

Be very, very, very, very careful when practicing anything neck-related. You can make somebody pass out from a neck hold like this one, and it would only take a short step and a bit of torque to break the neck. We are talking about self-defense, not homicide; if you can choose to knock the guy out as opposed to killing him, for Pete's sake, just knock him out. It's also self-defense to avoid a murder trial with you in the starring role.

Now you should have a reasonable understanding of joint-locking theory. Like everything else you have been shown so far, the only way to use joint locks to save your attractive butt is to practice until you can apply them smoothly, quickly, effortlessly, and viciously.

In the final sections of this handbook, you'll find descriptions of specific technical responses to various attack situations. Each response will involve some or all of the theory that has been expounded to date: blocking, targeted striking, breaking balance, and locking joints. Once you understand all the principles and can perform these things with technical correctness, you have learned your alphabet of self-defense.

When you become fluent in the choreographed techniques described in the next sections, you will understand how to turn that alphabet into words and sentences. Just as with language, once you get the alphabet, vocabulary, and an understanding of usage, you will be able to create freely on your own. I sincerely hope you never need to.

Lesson Four

LET GO!

Lesson Four

ESCAPING FROM GRABS

In this lesson, we will cover ways to escape from being grabbed. As women, we are less likely to get into a punch-'em-up at the local bar than men are. It is more likely that we will be in a situation where we are seized and restrained so the bad guy can get on with whatever nefarious activity he has in mind.

    Step 1: He grabs.
    Step 2: You kill him. No, no, no—sorry, too much caffeine.

Responding to a grab is counterintuitive (sound familiar?). When some big hairy guy closes his hands over you, unless you feel very fond of the lad, your first instinct is to pull away. The harder he grabs, the more you want to pull. Guess what? This is like trying to untie a knot by pulling really hard on the loose ends of the string. When you get grabbed, Step 2 is: *GO IN*. The first move you make is always to move in on your attacker. This has the effect of immediately loosening up his grip, and it will disconcert him.

    With any grab, it is important to initiate your technique the moment you feel the attacker make contact. The faster you act, the less time he will have to really latch onto you, or to resist or counter you if you are applying a controlling lock.

    Even if the attacker is much larger than you are, or you are not a particularly muscular specimen, you can make someone release you from a grab. Your weapons are strategic attacks to vulnerable body parts (remember the targets section), leverage, and—most important—knowledge. It is never just little you against big mean attacker. It is all of you knowing how to counterattack one small part of the bad guy.

Most of these grab releases will end up with your attacker off balance in some way, and often with him thrown to the ground. At that point, it is up to you to figure out if you need to stomp his face, kick in his ribs or his knees, or just run.

When you are ready to practice, please remember that if you are practicing with a male he will probably be invested in the notion that you can't really get away from him if he doesn't want you to. Remember Lesson 1; he'll probably feel this way even if he is an overtly politically correct fella, even if he is a really great guy. You are about to change the balance of power in your relationship. You ask him to grab you by the wrist and he applies the Grip of Death. He smiles confidently. "Okay," he says, "get out of that."

Poor male. Kick him in the shins. Now he will glare at you in outrage. "No fair," he'll say. When you point out that you are indeed now free of the grab, he'll accuse you of cheating. But what did he expect? Arm wrestling? Nonsense. You can let him know that you have been merciful—you did not kick him in the nuts or break his knee or any of his toes; you just moved his attention from his hands to his shins. Even if he didn't let go, you have caused his grip to loosen and your technique will work. We call this softening up the attacker.

To sum up, your technique for escaping from a grab will be:

1. Go in.
2. Soften up.
3. Apply leverage to release grip.
4. Inflict damage as necessary.
5. Go home.

SINGLE WRIST GRABS (FRONT)

Have your partner stand facing you. He should reach across to grab your right wrist with his right hand. Have his hand come down across the top of your wrist, so that his thumb wraps to the outside and his fingers wrap to the inside (an "opposite side" grab), see Figure 4-1.

Close your left hand over his right. Press your thumb against his index finger, holding it firmly in place against your forearm and his other

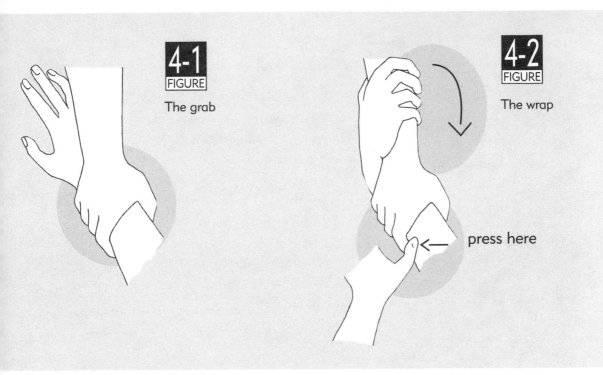

The grab

The wrap

←— press here

fingers. This makes it impossible for him to let go of you when his wrist starts to hurt. Oh darn.

Turn your right arm (tucking your elbow against your side will give you extra leverage) so that you now wrap your hand also around his wrist, with the edge of your hand positioned to press down into his forearm. Grab firmly onto his wrist with your right hand (Figure 4-2).

Have you ever started a motorcycle? A twist of your wrist is all it takes. Go slowly with your partner because when you get this right it will bring tears to his eyes, I promise. My eyes watered uncontrollably when I had one of my students do it to me, and I'm one tough old bird. Keeping his hand trapped with your left hand, use your right hand to pull his arm slightly toward you, twist it over, and press down and back toward his waist. You can use this to bring your partner all the way to the floor; once his knees buckle you can step backwards and pull the arm down to the ground (Figure 4-3). You may have to fool around a bit with this to make it work well, but when it works, believe me, you'll know it.

If your partner grabs your right hand with his left hand (a "same-side" grab), the technique works exactly the same way except that you wrap your hand around the outside of his forearm instead of the inside (Figure 4-4). Experiment with this until you can make it feel as nasty as the previous technique.

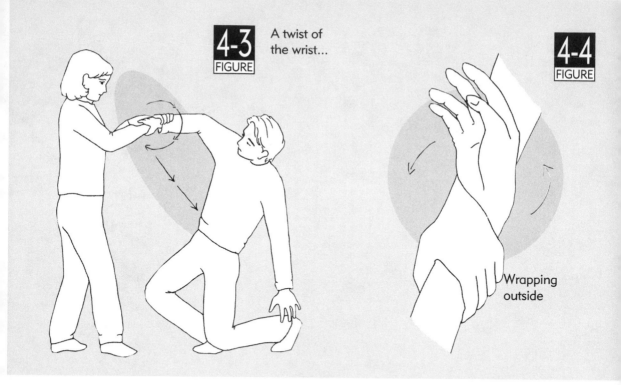

FIGURE 4-3 A twist of the wrist...

FIGURE 4-4 Wrapping outside

This particular wrist lock, when done correctly, will generate enough pain to keep your attacker immobile indefinitely. Remember, if you have to (for example, if you are down at the end of a deserted alley), you can apply enough pressure to mangle the wrist.

SINGLE WRIST GRAB (REAR)

If your attacker should grab your wrist from behind and yank it up between your shoulder blades, first try pulling down sharply with your forcarm. If he is holding your arm from the top, you should be able to step back toward him and simply yank down on your arm to get free. A rule of "thumb" if you will is always to go against the attacker's thumb instead of his four fingers, and if he is holding your arm from above, this is what you will do when you yank downward. However, if he knows his stuff, he will be supporting it from underneath.

Have your partner grab you this way, standing behind you with his right hand cupped under your right wrist and pulling it upward. If you are facing noon, step out to about two o'clock, straightening your elbow and leaning forward as necessary to relieve the pressure on your joints. This seems contrary to the "go in" rule, but we will forgive this minor trans-

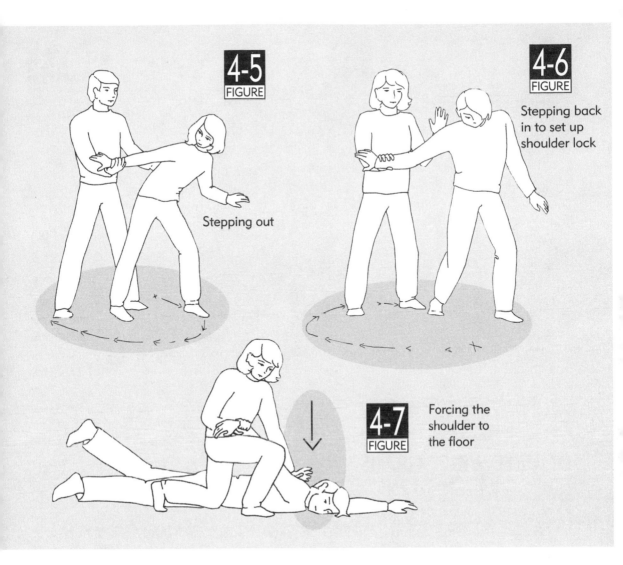

4-5 FIGURE

Stepping out

4-6 FIGURE

Stepping back in to set up shoulder lock

4-7 FIGURE

Forcing the shoulder to the floor

gression since, after you step out, you immediately turn around and step back in (Figure 4-5).

As your arms are extended between you, use the wrap from the single wrist grabs, curling your fingers around your partner's wrist and applying pressure to release his grip. Step back in and pull up on his wrist and push down on his shoulder (shoulder lock, previous lesson). As you can see, your right foot remained stationary, merely pivoting in place, as your left foot has made a neat semicircle on the floor (Figure 4-6).

As you apply downward pressure on the shoulder and upward pressure on the wrist, drop to your left knee, trapping the attacking arm against your right thigh. Keep pressure on the shoulder with your left hand (Figure 4-7). You will see that you can keep the attacker there as long as necessary.

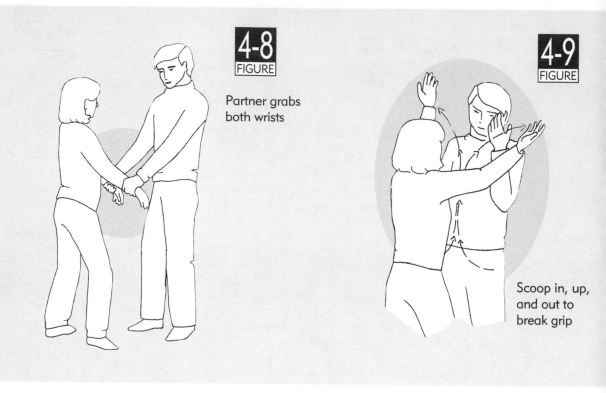

4-8 FIGURE

Partner grabs both wrists

4-9 FIGURE

Scoop in, up, and out to break grip

DOUBLE WRIST GRABS

Have your partner stand facing you. He should reach out and grab each of your wrists in his hands (Figure 4-8).

Step in toward your partner. (It doesn't matter on which foot.) Imagine reaching into an imaginary bucket, scooping up two big handfuls of water, and splashing them up into the air. Your hands scoop down, in, and then up. Keep your elbows tucked. The pressure of your forearm against your partner's thumb (rule of thumb, remember?) will become sufficient to cause him to release you. Sometimes you may have to extend your arms out to the sides before the leverage of your forearms against his thumbs causes the hold to break.

This is one technique where softening up may be very necessary, depending on the disparity between your strength and your partner/attacker's. If the attacker is concentrating on the grip, you need to take his attention away from his hands and put it elsewhere—his groin or his instep or his knee, or any of the handy pressure points and useful targets from Lesson 1. Also keep your movements loose and flowing; don't try to muscle your way out. Step in, drop your hands low into the imaginary bucket, and then lean back as you whip your arms upward

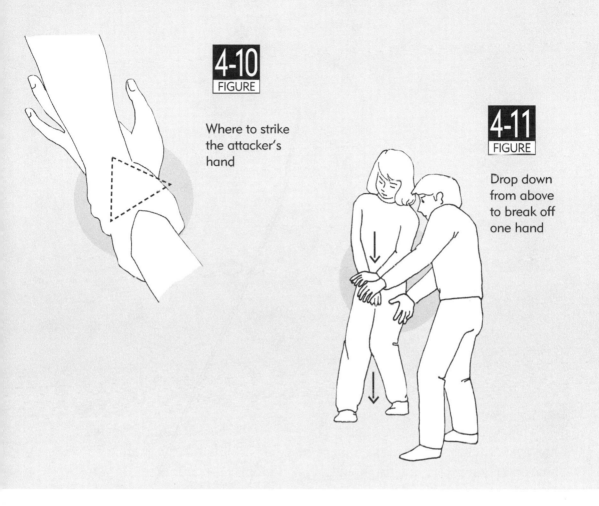

4-10
FIGURE

Where to strike
the attacker's
hand

4-11
FIGURE

Drop down
from above
to break off
one hand

(Figure 4-9). Remember to use your whole body; don't think about your hands only.

For a variation, have your partner grab both your wrists, as before. Sometimes the attacker will lock his elbows and is strong enough that you really can't get loose using the first technique (unless you really did smash his nuts). You should still be able to generate some lateral movement from those locked arms, though.

Step in. The possible softening-up options are still limited to your feet since your hands are trapped: groin, knees, inner thigh, instep. Now pivot on the ball of your left foot and drop like a ton of bricks with your right palm landing on the thumb joint of your partner's right hand, which holds your left wrist (Figure 4-10). Sink your knees as you drop your weight, and remember to stay loose and think heavy (Figure 4-11).

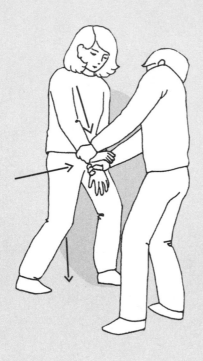

and then the other

This will free up your left hand. Drop down the heel of your left palm onto the attacker's left thumb joint if he is so foolish as to continue to hang on (Figure 4-12). This should happen quickly—blam! blam! If you find yourself not getting loose, step in closer, soften up more enthusiastically, and remember to get the feeling that all one-hundred-and-some pounds of you are landing on that one joint.

On the same theory, you can also try punching your right hand across your left so that the attacker's own hand whacks his other hand off your arm. Play around with this. This way you don't run the risk of getting any bruises at all, which is always nice.

LAPEL GRABS

A lapel grab means somebody has grabbed the front of your shirt. This doesn't happen much to women; it mostly happens to ten-year-old boys on the playground and Michael J. Fox in the *Back to the Future* movies. But you never know.

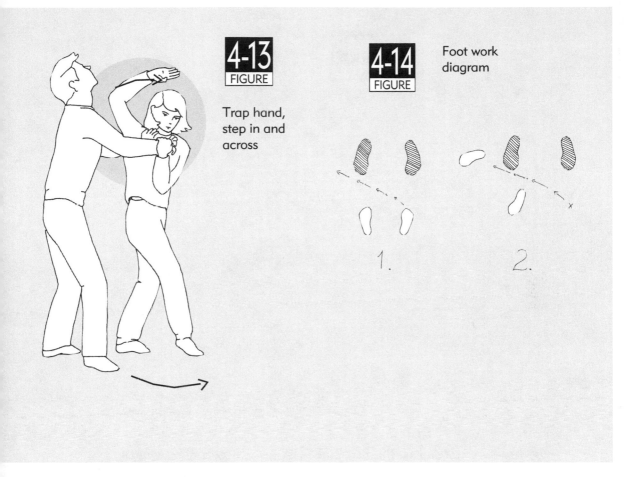

4-13 FIGURE

Trap hand, step in and across

4-14 FIGURE

Foot work diagram

1.

2.

Two-Hand Grab

(Note: This technique would not be good against a front choke because it doesn't relieve the pressure on your neck initially. In this case, you hope the attacker hangs on as tightly as possible.)

Have your partner grab handfuls of the front of your shirt. Your hands and your feet are going to work simultaneously. Your left hand closes over at least one of your partner's hands, trapping it more closely to you. Your right arm is going to come around and over your partner's arms in a swooping arc that cracks him in the jaw or the side of the face with your hand as it passes (Figure 4-13). That's the softening-up part.

Your right foot steps in and across, so that you end up in your horse stance with your back toward your partner (Figure 4-14). Sink your weight and keep his hands trapped against you. You will hear a thump off to your right side as he lands on the floor.

Trapping and pulling the attacker off balance

4-15 FIGURE

4-16 FIGURE

Trap and step back

If he does not fall to the floor, at least he will be pulled waaaay off balance to your right side and behind you (Figure 4-15). Immediately push off with your feet and drive your right elbow back into the attacker's face. If you are simply practicing, I implore you to look first or noses will be broken here.

One-Hand Grab

Have your partner reach out with his right hand and grab a handful of your shirt. Close your right hand over it, with your thumb pressing against the back and your fingers gripping the meaty part on the pinky side. If you remember how to do wrist locks, you will already know where we are going with this.

Flip the hand over. (If it is a big strong attacker, remember that you may have to soften up with a low kick first, and/or use your two hands to control the one grabbing hand.) Press the fingers back and down toward the elbow (see Lesson 3, Figures 3-9 and 3-10). Step back on your right foot. If you do this quickly and with enthusiasm, the attacker will hit the pavement nose-first. At least you can force him to bend over, and then you can kick him in the face and take off.

FRONT CHOKE

First of all, in a choke hold from the front, if the attacker can reach you, you can reach him. And if both his hands are around your neck, then, hey, both of yours are free. So softening up is a snap.

However, if he is choking you, you will need to move quickly before you pass out. Here are two different methods for dealing with an attacker who is choking you. For the first method, we can start with a modified version of the technique from Lesson 2, where the attacker was choking you as you lay on the floor. Now your escape is easier because you have a lot more freedom to put your body into your technique.

To begin, snake your right hand over the top of his left hand, and come up under his right arm with your palm facing outward. Now strike your left palm up against your right, fast and hard. At the same time, tuck your right elbow down against your side and *step back onto your right foot* (Figure 4-16). Stepping back is vital. It means your entire body weight is adding to the force of your forearm against the attacker's forearm. (Remember, it is never 143 pounds of you against a 205-pound attacker; it is 143 pounds of you against one little piece of the attacker—in this case, his arm.)

The attacker will go flying past you to your right, at which point you should have a sufficient window to run away. If his hands get trapped in your shirt instead, then at least he will be close enough for you to punch him in the face until he subsides. As he is off balance with his hands trapped, there's not much he can do about it—is there?

Another method to quickly relieve the pressure on your throat is to fold your arms across the top of the attacker's forearms. This is a separate technique, an alternative method for dealing with a choke. Snap out a quick instep kick to the groin or the inner thigh. (Since his hands are occupied I encourage you to go for the gusto here). Then, as you exhale, squeeze your folded arms toward your chest, trapping his arms underneath and leaving you standing like I Dream of Jeannie about to work magic (Figure 4-17). Your attacker will be on his knees in front of you. At

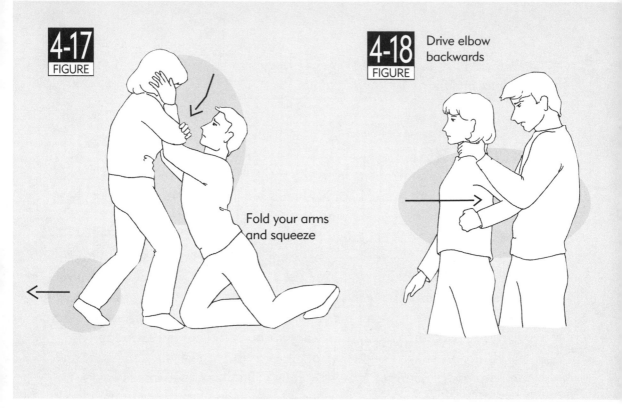

FIGURE 4-17

Fold your arms and squeeze

4-18 FIGURE Drive elbow backwards

this point you could knee him in the chest or snap out a kick to his groin, which will open your escape window nicely.

REAR CHOKE

A choke hold from behind would seem to present more difficulties in the softening-up arena, but don't forget, your attacker is still only arm's length away. Also, you can press backwards against him without putting pressure against the front of your throat, which gets you closer, if you feel you are too far away. And no matter how long your attacker's arms, your feet will always reach back far enough to do damage to his knees. You can also try bringing your heel up sharply to his groin; remember, his hands are full of your throat. With a particularly tall attacker, the groin shot may still be problematic, but you'll get his knees okay.

To begin, drive your right elbow back into the attacker's solar plexus (Figure 4-18). Then follow up with the edge of your right hand down into his groin (Figure 4-19). You don't need to see what you're doing; if your elbow drives into his stomach, his jewels are directly south, I assure you.

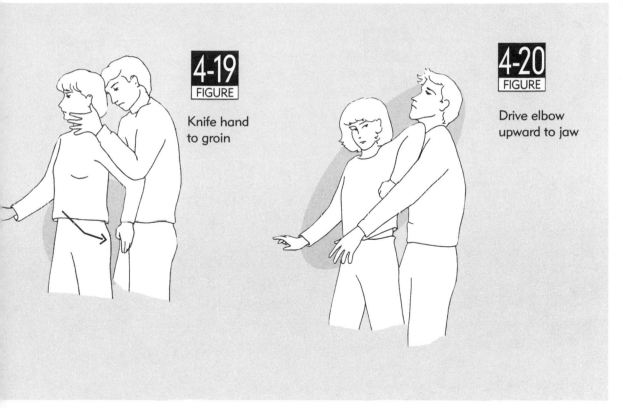

4-19 FIGURE

Knife hand
to groin

4-20 FIGURE

Drive elbow
upward to jaw

These two strikes will cause him to bend over at least a little, even if he's still hanging on to your neck. Step back toward him on your right foot and bring your elbow up behind you, into his chin (Figure 4-20).

This should loosen your attacker to the point where you can step around to face him completely. At this point I would continue with the arm that is already by his head (the right) and wrap his neck. From here you should know what to do, whether you want to break his neck or throw him to the floor. However, if you think the attacker is sufficiently groggy after the upward elbow to the chin, I would encourage you to head for the hills.

REAR SHOULDER GRAB

For the next technique against an attacker who has grabbed you by one or both shoulders, it is important to move your arm and foot at the exact same time. Raise up your right arm as though you are about to do the backstroke. Step behind you with your right foot, moving it diagonally behind you so that you are in the process of turning to face your attacker (Figure 4-21).

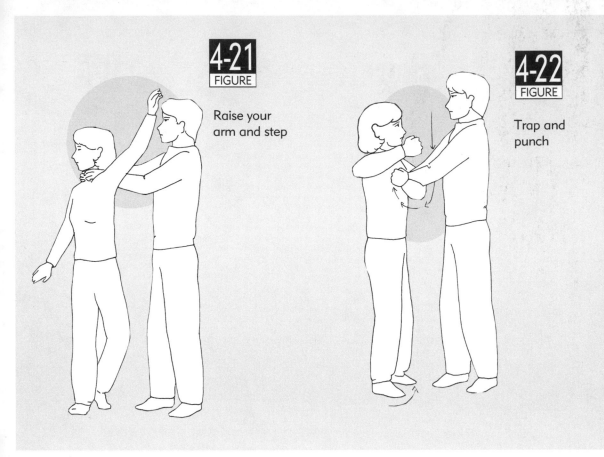

4-21 FIGURE — Raise your arm and step

4-22 FIGURE — Trap and punch

Bring your backstroking right arm down and across your attacker's arms as you turn your whole body around; this allows you to put your 143 pounds behind your moving arm and give it some oomph. Wrap your right arm tightly around his arms and hug them to you. Now deliver a snappy punch to his nose (Figure 4-22). If your first couple of punches don't do the job, switch to a low kick and take out his knee. Then run.

SIDE CHOKE

This choke is where the attacker wraps one arm around your neck and pulls you back against him, to the point where your weight is back on your heels and you are leaning against him. If he is pulling you back with his right arm, you are lying along the right side of his body and his right leg (Figure 4-23).

He thinks he's really got you, because you're off balance leaning against him. That's the part I like. First, turn your head so that the front of

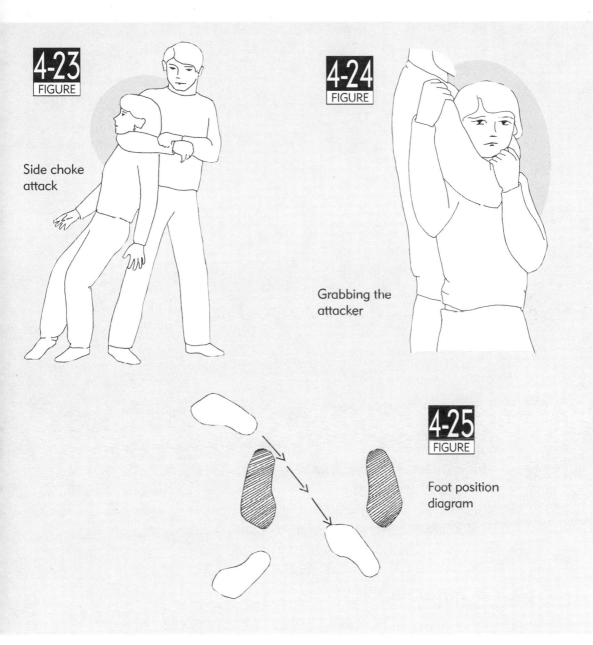

4-23 FIGURE

Side choke attack

4-24 FIGURE

Grabbing the attacker

4-25 FIGURE

Foot position diagram

your neck is in the crook of his elbow, and hook your left hand into his elbow and pull down to make sure you have air. Reach your right hand up and grab his shoulder (Figure 4-24). Latch on tightly.

Make sure your feet are positioned so that one is in front of his right foot and one is behind (Figure 4-25). Push back hard against him, *pushing off your left foot especially so that his weight moves back to his heels and he is off balance.* He is expecting you to pull away and struggle, so this is easy to do. He doesn't expect you to grab onto him and shove back.

Now, please remember all those sit-ups you have been doing EVERY DAY. Just crunch up your stomach muscles and yank down hard on his

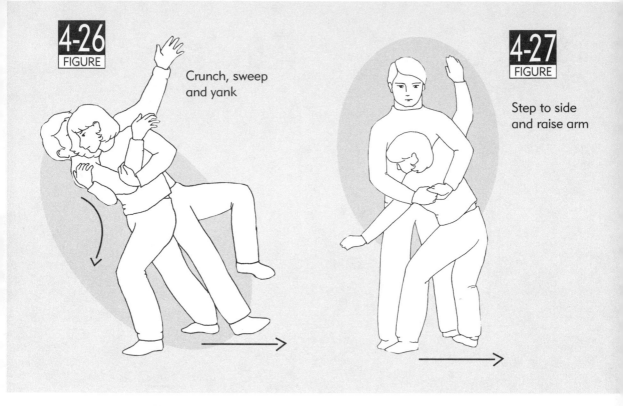

4-26 FIGURE

Crunch, sweep and yank

4-27 FIGURE

Step to side and raise arm

arm and shoulder (Figure 4-26). At the same time, sweep your right foot back against his right leg, knocking that foot out from under him. He will come flying to the floor in front of you.

While he's lying there stunned, kick him in the head or whatever part is convenient, and then run. Are you sensing a pattern here?

BEAR HUG (FRONT)

Luckily, a bear hug is one of those grabs that you can see coming. If the guy is much stronger than you, you will have to be good at softening him up. With your arms pinned at your sides, you can still certainly bring your knee up into his groin, or drill your knuckles into those tender points on the side along the ribs. If he's not a lot taller, whap your forehead into his nose.

Once you have got his grip a bit softer, step to the side with your right foot, lift up your right arm, and tuck your head down to the left, with your face toward the floor (Figure 4-27).

Bend your body over toward the left as you step to the right, with your right arm pushing up against the attacker's left arm (Figure 4-28). The attacker's arm slides up and across the back of your head. This is why

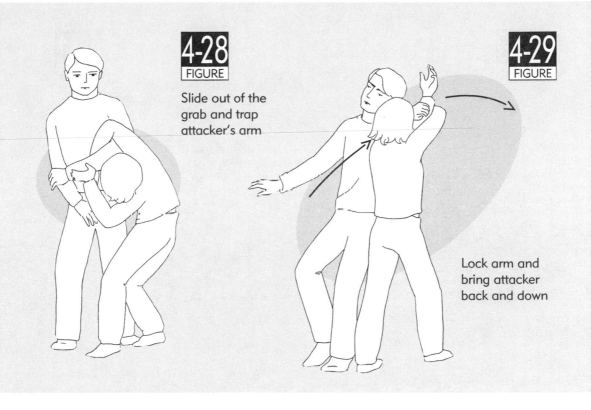

Slide out of the grab and trap attacker's arm

Lock arm and bring attacker back and down

you turn your face down to the floor; you don't want his arm snagging on your ear or your nose.

Take your left arm and come up from under the attacker's left arm. Fold it back over your right arm and grab your left forearm in your right hand, in that triangular trap that will be familiar from the joint lock section (Figure 4-29). With the attacker's arm trapped in yours, walk toward your attacker, staying well to the side, and bring him over backwards to the floor. Bring him down hard so that you hit him with the floor, which will stun him.

BEAR HUG (REAR)

Okay, so you can't see this one coming. Softening-up options include stomping backwards onto his knee or instep. If you have enough mobility in your forearms (assuming your upper arms are probably trapped against you), snap the edge of your hand down and backwards into his groin (Figure 4-30). You can even claw down there and grab a healthy handful of whatever presents itself.

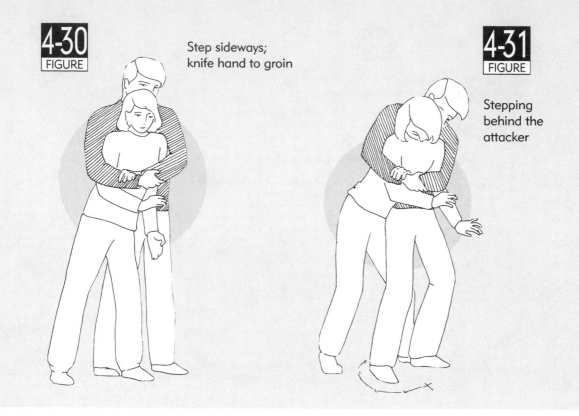

FIGURE 4-30

Step sideways;
knife hand to groin

FIGURE 4-31

Stepping
behind the
attacker

While he is thinking about protecting his nuts, you should move your hips to the right, and then *slide your left foot all the way around his right foot and end up with it behind him* (Figure 4-31). You will find that you have to bend forward to accomplish this. When you bend forward your attacker will just hang on even tighter. Oh darn again.

Now it is a simple matter to use those long, strong thigh muscles. Push off the floor and straighten up, corkscrewing your shoulders back and to the left. This knocks your attacker backwards over your left leg, which you positioned behind him as you stepped back (Figure 4-32).

HEAD LOCK

Okay, okay, it's another situation that is more likely to happen to Michael J. Fox than to any of you. I'm including it as an example of using your brains to defeat your opponent's brawn, and because it's elegant and effective.

For the attack, have your partner stand next to you, facing the same direction as you. He should now put his near arm around your neck and

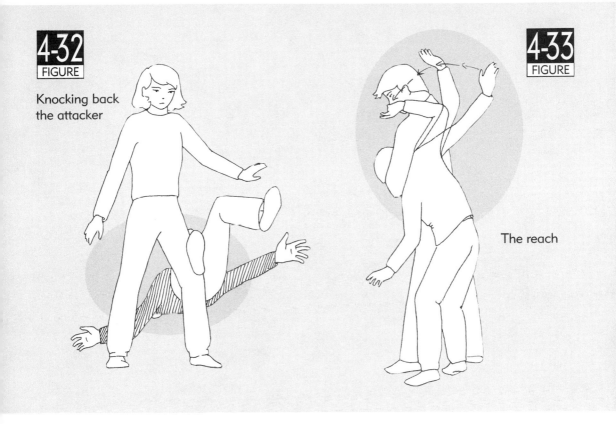

4-32 FIGURE

Knocking back
the attacker

4-33 FIGURE

The reach

pull your head down against his side so that your ear winds up somewhere in the vicinity of his floating ribs. He is welcome to use his free hand to grab his forearm and crank on the grab.

First, soften him up. Since you are looking right at the groin, the knees, and the inner thighs, I hope you have enough imagination to figure out a way to do this. Now, take your right hand and reach behind you, then up between your head and his (Figure 4-33). Slide your hand across the near side of his head, using the Braille method to get your two fingers pressed into the sensitive area between his upper lip and nose (Figure 4-34).

Push *back* and *down*, pressing against the underside of the nose. If you move your arm quickly, with force, your opponent ends up on the floor. In the unlikely event that your opponent does NOT let go of your neck, you end up on top of him and in a favorable position to do damage and run away. I have not yet had anyone not let go when pressure is correctly targeted and applied, though.

This one is so simple and effective that it is a good parlor trick if you ever want to show off your "skills." It's sort of like never-fail instant pudding.

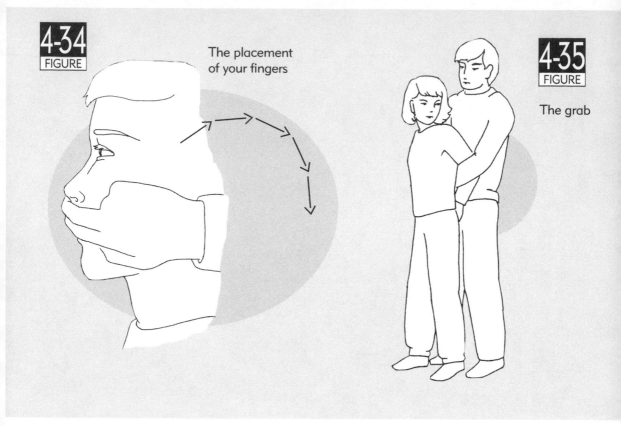

The placement
of your fingers

The grab

REAR ARM TRAP

Have your partner stand behind you, grabbing your arms at about the elbow and pulling them backwards (Figure 4-35). Have him hold your arms as tightly as he can. As always, the technique works best against someone who is hanging on in the Grip O' Death.

Soften up the attacker by grabbing straight south (Braille method) and giving a healthy twist, squeeze, and yank. (If your partner is a woman, you will be need to use your imagination, duh. By the way, if your attacker really is a woman, even we don't like the edge of someone's hand driven back hard into our sensitive bits.)

Next, pull your arms against you to trap the attacker's hands and forearms even more thoroughly. You don't want him letting go until you have hit him with the floor. Drop to your left knee, crunching your stomach muscles and curling in your left shoulder toward your center. You can use your right knee and right shoulder, whichever feels more natural. Push up with your right elbow as you are dropping and crunching (Figure 4-36). Your attacker will head for the floor, top of his head first. In the unlikely event that he does not let go in an attempt to break his fall, keep rolling so that at least you will land on top of him on

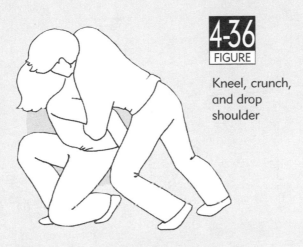

Kneel, crunch,
and drop
shoulder

your back. Do so with enthusiasm and vigor, banging your head back into his nose and driving your heel up into his groin or stomping down onto his knee. He'll let go.

BEAR HUG (REAR, NO ARMS)

It's possible that an attacker could try to grab you around the waist to lift you and carry you off to the waiting van or nearest dark alley. It's actually rather difficult to strike backwards at someone who has you picked up off the floor and held tight against him, if he tucks his head off to one side so you can't toss your head back and give him a broken nose. Other than that, or kicking viciously back at his legs, you are in a bit of a quandary once you are out of contact with the floor.

Have you ever tried to lift a sleepy three-year-old out of a car seat? The kid seems to have gained four hundred and twelve pounds, right? This is because you have to reach in over the car seat. I'm sure your chiropractor has told you about using your legs and keeping your back straight to lift. So we use this principle when someone tries to lift us from behind (Figure 4-37). The first step is to dive out and down, splaying your legs and arms wide, the minute you feel someone's arms around you from behind (Figure 4-38). If it's your beloved, well, you can always stand back up.

At this point, often your grabber will have to let go. You can skitter forward like a bug on your hands and feet until you can take off

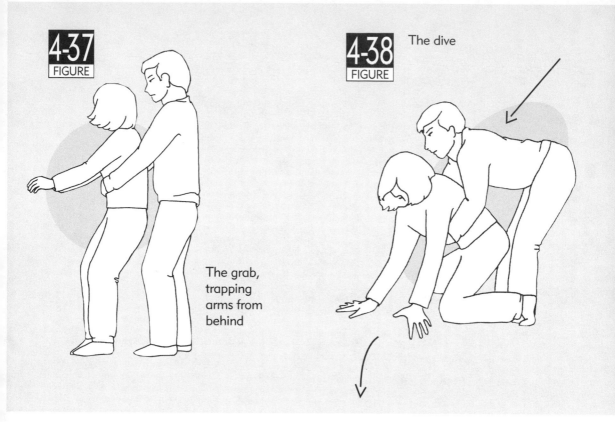

4-37 FIGURE

The grab, trapping arms from behind

4-38 FIGURE — The dive

running (Monty Python defense). But for the sake of amusement, we will go to the worst-case scenario and assume that he hangs on tight.

As you dive, don't just dive straight forward; angle your dive off to one side. When you glance back through your splayed knees, if the attacker is hanging on tight, you will see one of his feet. Shove backwards with your butt hard against his knee as you reach between your thighs and grab the foot (Figure 4-39). You will probably have to be moving backwards anyway to reach the foot. Lock your fingers around behind his heel or ankle.

Now drop your weight back and down on your butt—and therefore on your attacker's knee—and pull up hard on his foot (Figure 4-40). The leverage on his leg will force him to let go of you; the longer he waits to let go and the more force and leverage you use, the more likely it is that his knee will make an ugly little popping sound and be of no use at all for some time to come.

These are not, by any stretch of the imagination, the only possible technical responses to the various grabs, and indeed, these are not the

4-39 FIGURE Shove against knee; grab foot

4-40 FIGURE

Pull up on foot and sit down on leg

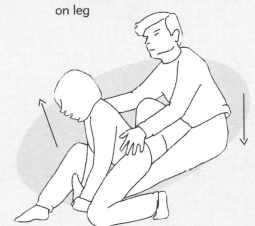

only ways the bad guy can grab you. However, as you grasp the principles that make these responses effective, you can figure out how to get out of any grab. Experiment with your partner and see what you can figure out for yourself.

Just remember: Don't panic. Go in. Soften up. Use leverage to break grips and lock joints. Inflict damage. Go home. Eat some chocolate. Watch a sunset.

Lesson Five

CLUB
DEFENSE

Lesson Five

A club is any big stick or baseball bat type of weapon. It can be wood, metal, or some other unyielding substance. It doesn't matter what it's made of, because with a bit of practice it will never come into contact with your personal body. Please remember, however, that a person with a weapon is more dangerous than one without, which means that you should try your hardest to find a way to avoid a confrontation, no matter how much practice you have under your belt.

MOMENTUM AND RANGE

To successfully defeat an attacker who is armed with a club, there are two factors that you will need to understand and use. The first is the *range* of the weapon. A stick will extend the bad guy's sphere of influence by about three feet (or whatever the length of the stick may be). You are no longer safe when you are standing four feet from your assailant, which is outside of effective punchy-kicky distance. However, the silver lining to this particular cloud is that there is now a window of relative safety directly up against your attacker (Figures 5-1 and 5-2). A stick is not a good weapon when you are very close, unless your attacker is interested in giving you a bit of a poke with it.

A club becomes a significant threat if it has had a chance to develop *momentum*, that is, to be in motion for a sufficient length of time so that it gathers enough speed to be dangerous. The longer a club has been in motion, the harder it will be to stop and the more it will hurt if

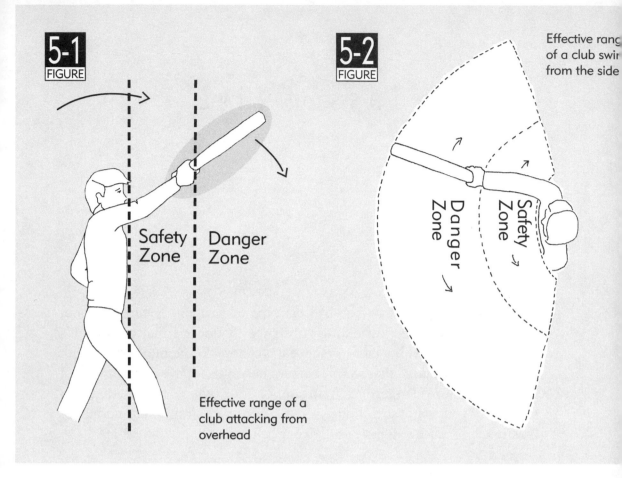

FIGURE 5-1

Safety Zone | Danger Zone

Effective range of a club attacking from overhead

FIGURE 5-2

Effective range of a club swing from the side

Danger Zone | Safety Zone

it hits you. Therefore, the bad guy's attack will be an attempt to create the maximum momentum. Your response will be to use that momentum, not to fight against it. You will encourage it along its original path (or a slightly altered one) vigorously. Momentum is your friend. It is one of your weapons even when you are barehanded. The bigger the bad guy is and the faster he comes in, the better the following techniques will work.

When the attacker moves to strike with a club, whether striking down at your head or sideways at your body, he swings the weapon from behind him to out in front of him where you are standing. The sooner you interrupt this swing, the easier it will be to control. Always try to get inside the safety zone and get your hands on the attacker's arm, before the weapon has broken the plane in which the attacker's body lies (Figures 5-3 and 5-4). This way, the gathering momentum will be under your control.

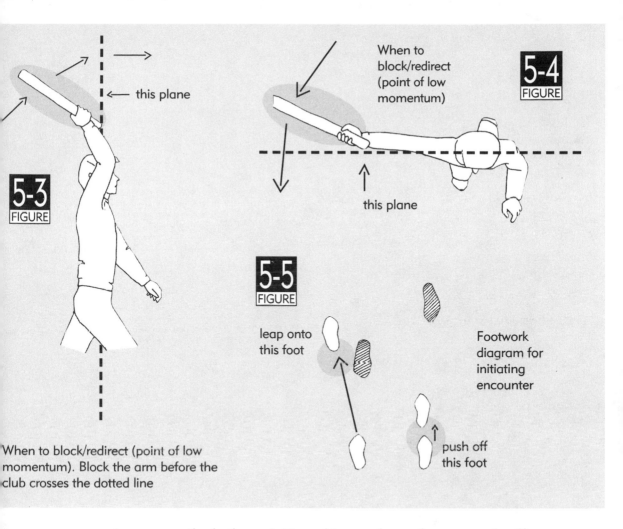

this plane

When to block/redirect (point of low momentum)

this plane

leap onto this foot

Footwork diagram for initiating encounter

push off this foot

When to block/redirect (point of low momentum). Block the arm before the club crosses the dotted line

As soon as the bad guy initiates his attack you have to push off your rear leg and spring in toward him. Does the word *counterintuitive* sound familiar here?

OVERHEAD CLUB DEFENSE

The Footwork

Be sure that you practice the techniques in this section from the appropriate starting point. No fair facing your partner with your feet already in the safety zone! Start about four feet apart. When your partner steps in on the attack, you should really have to leap in to counter. Both your feet should move. You push off your left foot and spring onto your right (or vice versa), but your forward foot should move so far that your rear foot gets dragged forward several inches, as you can see in Figure 5-5. Practice this leaping in several times before moving on to the techniques.

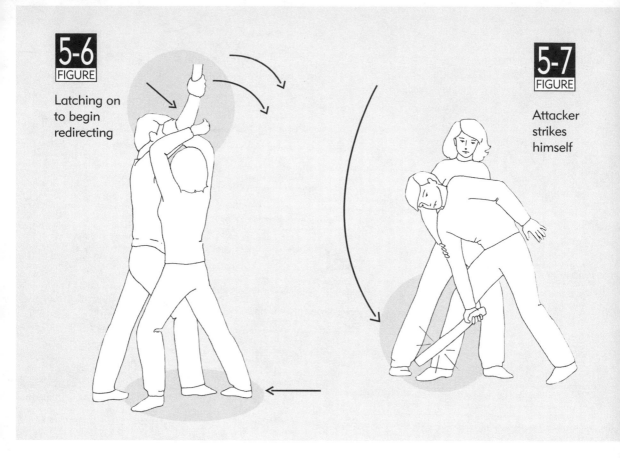

The Techniques

For the first technique, have your partner hold the club in his right hand, standing with his left foot forward. He should step in onto his right foot, bringing the club up over his head and in a downward direction toward your head (as though you are a railroad spike and he is going to pound you into the ground). You should initially be standing four to five feet away, right in the effective range window.

Push off on your right foot, bringing both arms up so that your forearms overlap above your forehead, right arm over left. Your left foot should land to the outside of your partner's right (forward) foot, with your body turned toward your partner. Your arms create a protective curve directly above your forehead, which will deflect the attack even if you flub the rest of the technique (Figure 5-6).

As you feel your partner's arm come into contact with yours, latch your hands onto it and pull down and to your right. Aim it so that either the club passes between his legs and he whacks himself in the groin with his own arm, or it strikes him on the shin (Figure 5-7).

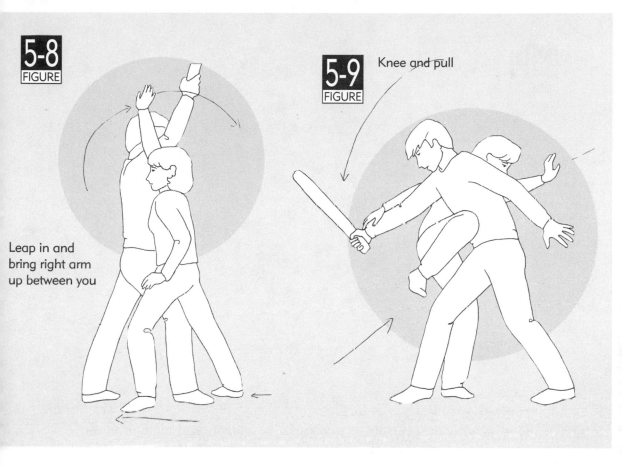

5-8 FIGURE

Leap in and bring right arm up between you

5-9 FIGURE Knee and pull

As you can see, the faster and harder the attack, the more force the attacker strikes himself with. (Momentum! Tah dah!) At this point, it is generally possible to recover the club from the attacker and do some whacking of your own.

For the second technique, have your partner attack in precisely the same way as the first technique. You will also initiate your response in the same way, by pushing off on the right foot and landing with your left foot to the outside of your partner's right. This time, however, you should keep your body facing forward and swing your right arm forward and up between you (Figure 5-8).

As your left foot lands, keep your right arm swinging back and around (making a sweeping vertical circle). Your right arm will come down onto your partner's arm, pulling him down onto your right knee, which you are driving up into his solar plexus (Figure 5-9). Your partner will find himself nearly impaled on your knee. Use consideration; it's easy to hit him too hard.

As the attacker is whooping and puking on the sidewalk from having the wind (and maybe the lunch) knocked out of him, bring your right

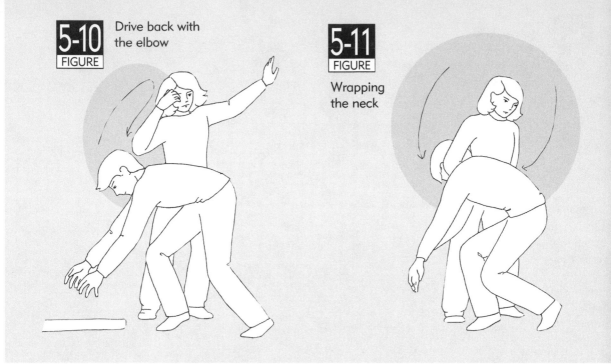

FIGURE 5-10 Drive back with the elbow

FIGURE 5-11 Wrapping the neck

elbow back down sharply against the base of his skull (Figure 5-10). This is likely to send him face forward onto the pavement, and should allow you a large enough window through which to run away. If it does not, you can wrap the neck (Figure 5-11) and throw your attacker, break the neck, or choke him out, as discussed previously.

If at any point during these techniques the attacker loses his grip on the club, of course you should grab it. But you should also note that none of these defenses ever call for you to make contact with the weapon. Your bare arm against a sturdy piece of nerveless wood is a bad bet. Always make sure you are blocking and redirecting the attacker's arm, not the weapon itself.

With practice you will get the attacker to flow from attacking you into crashing himself without any hesitation.

SIDE CLUB DEFENSE

The same theory works for a club attack that is coming in like Babe Ruth swatting a fast ball. Now that the attack is coming in laterally, in order to take advantage of the momentum, you'll redirect laterally also. Once again, it is important to get ahold of the attacking arm before it breaks the plane in which the body is standing (Figure 5-12).

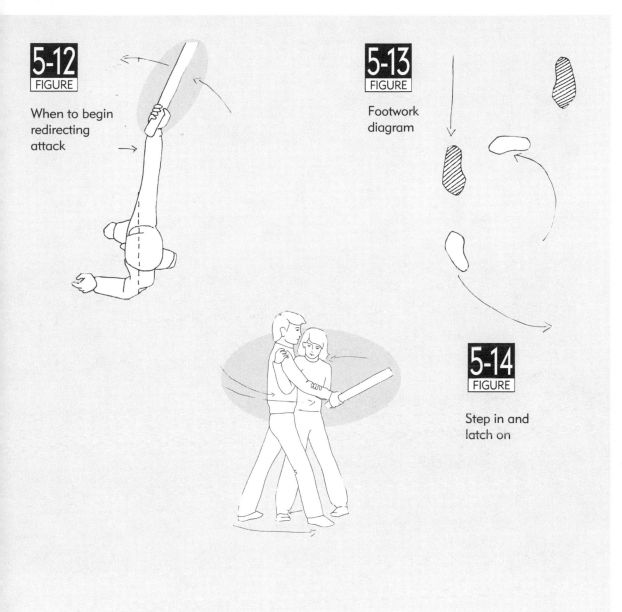

5-12
FIGURE

When to begin
redirecting
attack

5-13
FIGURE

Footwork
diagram

5-14
FIGURE

Step in and
latch on

For the first technique, your partner should hold the club in his right hand. As he steps in on his right foot, he swings the club parallel to the floor at the height of your ribs, in a one-handed version of a baseball bat swing. As his right foot lands, you push off on your left foot and land in between his feet with your right foot (Figure 5-13).

Turn so that your back is against his front as you step. Bring your right arm up under his attacking arm and latch onto his shoulder, as you did in the defense against a side choke in the previous chapter. Grip his shoulder tightly. Your left hand grabs lower down on his arm, anywhere around the elbow (Figure 5-14). Step out on your left foot

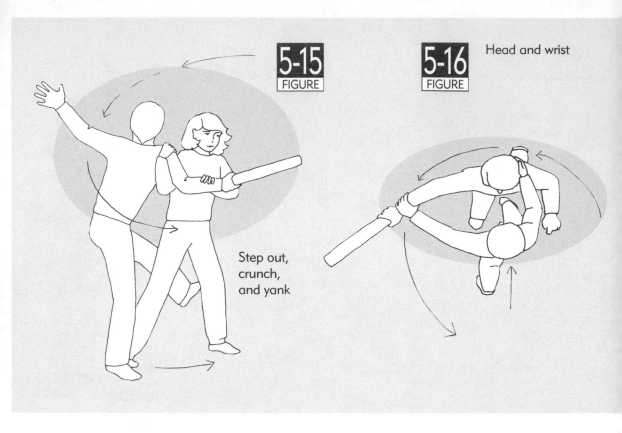

Head and wrist

Step out,
crunch,
and yank

and keep pulling him around in the direction he was already going. (Can you say "momentum"?) While you are stepping, crunch down and yank as you did in that same side choke defense (Figure 5-15), and he will roll away from you along the floor for quite a distance. This should give you plenty of time to take off. Practicing the footwork will feel almost like dancing.

For the second technique, the attack and the footwork are identical to the first technique. Your right arm comes up to the outside of the attacker's head, though, and your left hand grabs the attacker's right wrist (Figure 5-16).

As you pull down on the wrist, push on his head so that you are pressing his far ear into his shoulder. Maintain this pressure as you step back on your left foot, as previously, and pull sharply on his right arm (Figure 5-17). The attacker will hurtle headfirst into the floor—as you know, where one part of the body is directed, the rest willfollow. You should feel as though you are steering the attacker headfirst into the floor.

FIGURE

Step and pull

As with the grab techniques, these are certainly not the only possible things to do when someone attacks you with a club. I emphasize these techniques because they do not require a lot of muscle; you only need to understand the principles that make them work.

When these techniques get very smooth, it will seem as though you are the eye of the hurricane, and the attacker flings himself at you and is repelled by a force of nature. Another way to look at it—He's the s*** and you're the fan. You know what happens when the one hits the other. Not elegant, but vivid, isn't it?

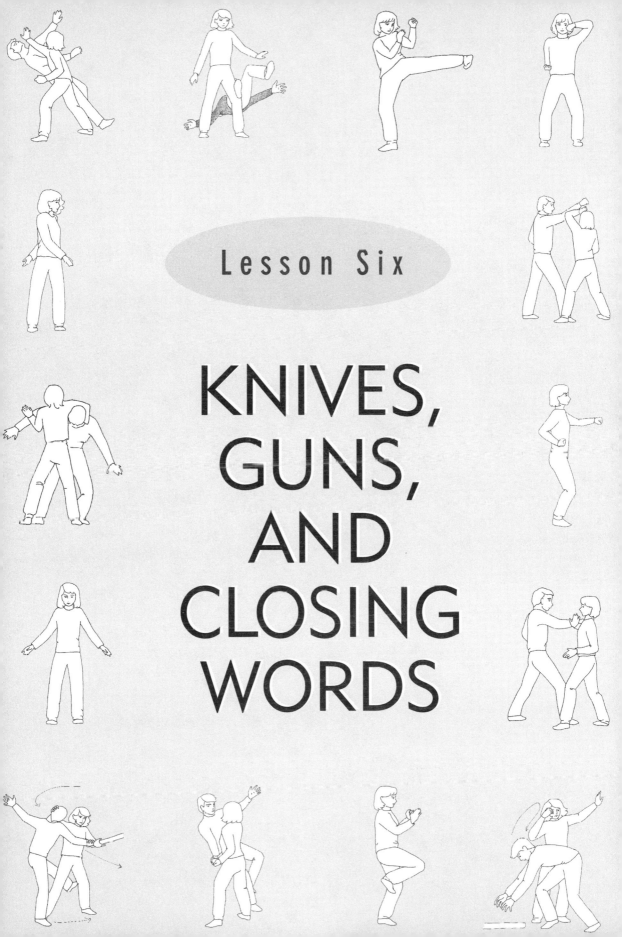

Lesson Six

KNIVES, GUNS, AND CLOSING WORDS

Lesson Six

KNIFE DEFENSE

Knives are nastier than clubs, and perhaps even nastier than guns. A gun is only dangerous in one direction, and then only if the attacker has the skill and presence of mind to aim it correctly. A knife can stab or slash from any angle, in any direction. If you are within arm's length of the attacker, you're in trouble. This means that the first thing we work on in knife defense is range, especially in terms of staying out of it.

PRACTICE DRILLS FOR RANGE

Dodging the Attacker

Stand facing your partner, just out of reach. Every time your partner moves toward you, adjust your feet so that you are still out of reach. You must stay facing your partner (you don't want to turn your back on a guy with a knife). You can only step back so many times until you run into a wall, so practice ducking and sidestepping as well, especially if your partner tries to charge you. You should feel like you and your partner are magnets with the wrong ends facing, so that his movements cause you to fly away from him.

When you feel like you're getting good at this exercise, have your partner try to touch you, instead of just close the distance. When you get touched (and you will, pretty quickly), then it is your turn to try to tap your partner.

Finally, have your partner deliberately try to maneuver you into a corner as he goes for you. Don't let him. You will have to be very quick on your feet to stay "alive" in this drill for long.

Using Impromptu Weapons

If you should find yourself facing a person with a knife, you do not want to be barehanded if at all possible. Look around you for anything you can throw: rocks, a handful of dirt, your car keys, anything else heavy in your bag or pocket. (Do you have a hairbrush? Wallet? Remember, things are all replaceable. Your internal organs are not.) Pick up more than one thing—if you miss with the first you have backups. Don't wait to see if you got him the first time; throw the second and third things anyway. Throw hard, and aim at his face.

Please note, this is appropriate for *any* attack situation, against either a bare-handed opponent *or* one wielding a weapon. Everything is fair game if you are being attacked.

As you walk down the street, even in broad daylight and complete safety, play "what if." What if a guy with a knife is behind that mailbox? What can I throw at him? Be creative—you could even throw your shoes if you had to, couldn't you? It doesn't matter how silly you look, it matters that you—what? Oh, yeah. GET HOME SAFELY.

Using Impromptu Shields

The next step is to assume that you couldn't throw anything, or you missed him, or he doesn't seem to mind being hit in the face with a rock. As he closes the distance you must find some way to shield yourself. Is there a garbage can with a lid nearby? Grab it, and to hell with germs. Do you carry a pocketbook the size of a small suitcase? Use it to intercept the knife. Take off your jacket and wrap it around your left forearm, assuming you are right-handed. You want to blunt the attack with your left and go for his face with your right. You will probably get cut, but if you can break his nose or gouge him in the eyes, you will also probably get away. Once again, think of your shoes—put them on your hands, and block with one and hit him in the face with your fist encased in the other.

Be creative.

PRACTICE TECHNIQUES
FOR DEFENSE AGAINST KNIVES

Should you end up going barehanded against a knife, you'll need to control the weapon. Focus on your attacker as you did in the blocking drills earlier, so that you are aware of any movement as soon as it starts. As the attacker moves toward you, you have to latch onto the attacking arm, immobilize it (remember joint locks?), and then neutralize the attack. Specifically, do not look at the knife itself; it is possible to become somewhat mesmerized at the sight, and then your responses will be too slow. Always keep a soft focus on the entire attacker.

Straight-In Knife Attack

For the first technique, have your partner step in toward you and stab forward toward your bellybutton with a practice knife of any sort. Use something that won't hurt you if you mess up the technique. Toy stores don't even sell good rubber knives anymore; you have to buy an entire G.I. Joe Commando Kit and throw out the grenades and the plastic soldier vest. And take it from me, the little binoculars are a total ripoff. You can hardly ever see out of both eyes at once.

I actually found a rubber knife lying in a parking lot, and it was a really good one, with a compass concealed in the handle and everything. If your child lost such a thing some time in the spring of 1998 in the parking lot at Ricki's Florist, please give me a call. In the meantime, it's getting a lot of use. But once again, I digress.

Step on your left foot to the outside of your partner's attacking arm, parrying the knife past you and grabbing onto his wrist with your right hand. Really grab on. You should feel as though you are in familiar territory if you have been practicing your techniques regularly; all we are doing is modifying the technique from Lesson 2 into a knife defense technique. This doesn't mean that there aren't any other good techniques. I just want you to start to think about using what you know instead of worrying about what you don't know.

Strike hard to the ribs with your left elbow as you step under the attacking arm, turning your back to your partner and rotating his hand palm up. Bring your left hand up to grab onto your partner's hand from the other side, which will help you rotate it fully. See where we are now?

Do you remember what to do next? Of course you do! Kneel down and pull his hand onto the floor by your feet.

If you like variety, as you practice you can also see how it would work to yank the arm down across your shoulder without kneeling down. If you have turned the hand palm-up, the elbow will be bent in a way it is not supposed to be. If this was really a knife-wielding bad guy, you could just go ahead and snap that joint like a well-cooked drumstick.

For the second technique, have your partner stab in as before. Step back on your right foot, sucking in your stomach and curving your spine outward into as much of a "C" shape as you can manage. Slam down on top of the attacking arm just at the wrist with your crossed forearms (Figure 6-1). Make sure you have sucked your stomach back far enough that the knife won't touch you. Practice with any pretend weapon and have your partner really try to get you. Don't go any further with this technique until you consistently get the block right.

Next, as you block, make sure your right hand is on top. As soon as you make contact with the attacker's arm, clamp your hands down on his wrist and seize the meaty parts of his hand. Your right hand will grasp the pinky side of the attacking hand, and your left hand will clamp onto the ball of the thumb. Flip the hand over and apply pressure so that the fingers

Reverse
blocking and
setting up for
wrist lock

go back toward the elbow and the attacker bends forward—the classic
wrist lock.

See Lesson 3 (Figures 3-9 and 3-10) for the illustration and any
necessary reviews of the workings of wrist locks. Can you tell that I am
trying to show you how the stuff you already know is what you need to
defend against an attack?

Once the attacker is bent double from the pressure on his wrist, you
can kick him in the face until he passes out. Because he's bent over, the
high-kick rule doesn't count—you only need to kick about knee height,
since that's where his face is. And if the guy is attacking you with a knife,
don't even think about restraining him and yelling for help. Put the sucker
out. Repeated blows will have a cumulative effect; don't go looking for that
one-strike-kill thing.

For the third technique, have your partner attack as before, stabbing
in toward your stomach. Make your well-practiced block from the
previous technique. Please note that in these three knife techniques all the
blocks come with footwork, either side-stepping like in Technique 1, or
drawing back as in 2 and 3. This time make sure your left hand is on top,
gripping the attacker's hand as you block (Figure 6-2). Use your right
forearm as a lever, and roll your right arm from the shoulder as you tuck
your left elbow into your side (Figure 6-3). Step back. Pull. This technique is reminiscent of the lemmings takedown technique where you
caught the punch on your right and then flipped it over to your left like
steering a race car. See how the puzzle pieces fit . . . .

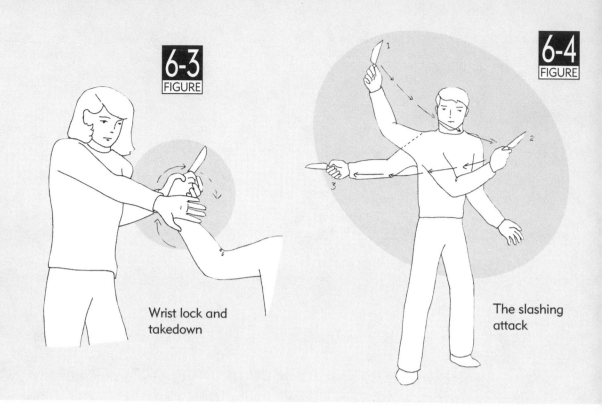

Wrist lock and takedown

The slashing attack

If this was a real attack, you would proceed to break the wrist and do anything else damaging and immobilizing that presented itself. When you have your partner on the floor, see what occurs to you.

Slashing Knife Attack

For this attack, the partner should step in on his right foot, slashing with the knife from right to left and then back from left to right—like Zorro but without the final line on the Z (Figure 6-4).

Step back on your left foot, allowing the first strike to go past you. Immediately push off on the left foot and leap in, stopping the returning strike even as it starts (Figure 6-5). Remember momentum? Breaking the plane? The sooner you get your hands on this slash, the easier it will be to stop. Get both of your hands pushing up against the attacking arm (Figure 6-6).

Next, wrap your left arm over your partner's biceps muscle and down across the crease of his elbow (Figure 6-7). Your right forearm rolls under the arm and pushes back, folding the arm in half across your left arm. Your left hand reaches through to grab and support your own right forearm in the

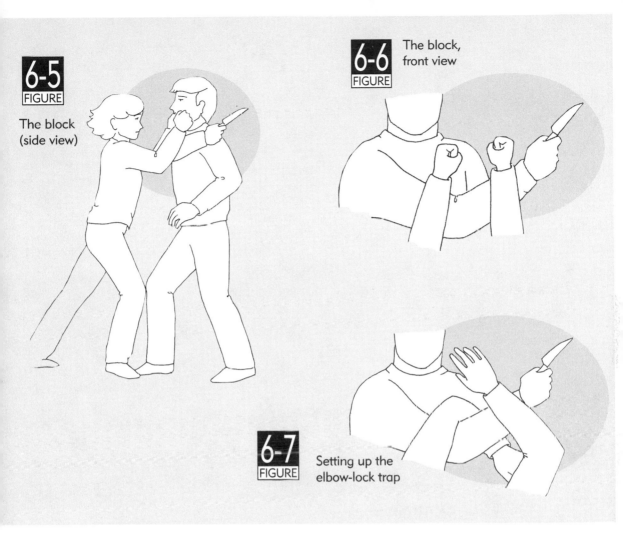

6-5 FIGURE

The block (side view)

6-6 FIGURE

The block, front view

6-7 FIGURE

Setting up the elbow-lock trap

triangle trap (Figure 6-8) as we practiced in—Tah dah!—the joint locks section! I love it when a plan comes together.

You will find that you have sufficient control of the attacking arm and ergo the knife to force the attacker to slash his own face or neck at this time. It sounds bloodthirsty, but in a "him or you" situation, I urge you to choose YOU.

To try a different version, use the same attack and same block as before. This time, wrap your right hand around the ball of the thumb of the attacking hand. Bring your left hand under the attacking hand and grab from underneath at the meaty part on the pinky side. Step underneath the arm (Figure 6-9). Surprise! You end up in the correct position to either break the arm over your shoulder or slam the wrist down onto the floor, as in the straight-in knife technique that came from the lemmings takedown section in Lesson 2.

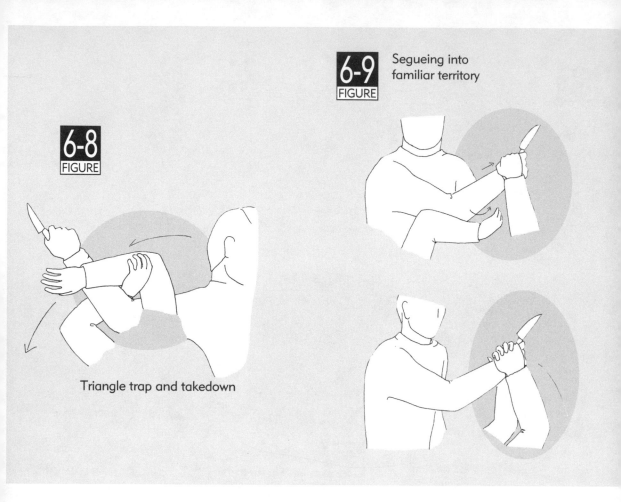

6-8
FIGURE

6-9
FIGURE

Segueing into familiar territory

Triangle trap and takedown

Downward Knife Attack

Should the bad guy attack by slashing down at you with the knife point downward, sidestep as in the overhead club attack and pull his hand down into his own thigh. This works exactly the same way as when you redirected the club into his shins.

Like learning words that you fit together to make sentences appropriate to many occasions, you will begin gradually to recognize your vocabulary of skills in all of these defense techniques. Think about modifying other things you have learned, to respond to all of these kinds of attacks. Look, you're speaking self-defense.

THE ULTIMATE KNIFE DEFENSE PRACTICE DRILL

So, you think you know how to defend against a knife? Try this.

Put on your oldest sweatpants and T shirt. Give your partner a wide-point, washable, humongo-sized marker. Tell him to attack you like he really means it—any attack at all—vigorously.

Defend yourself for about thirty seconds and then look in the mirror. Your shirt will be covered with lines. You will probably have more of them on your arms and hands. Thank your lucky stars that none of it is blood. Now go practice your techniques some more. It will take weeks and weeks of concentrated practice before you can keep your partner from drawing all over you, practically at will. But this should give you a new and healthy respect for that knife-wielding attacker. Remember, if you can run away, it is always your first best line of defense to do so, no matter how many courses you've taken or how much you think you know.

GUN DEFENSE

As I mentioned in the beginning of the knife section, I'd rather face a gun than a knife. Guns require maximum skill on the part of the attacker, and minimum skill on your part. However, if you are shot, recovering from a gunshot may be worse and more prolonged than recovering from a cut. But recovering from either is better than not recovering at all.

In discussing defense against guns, momentum is not the main factor—range is. Here are three possible scenarios:

1. The guy is down the street (more than twenty feet away), pointing a gun at you. Your response: Dart for cover, weaving and staying low. Keep moving and stay behind things. Make a lot of commotion, sound any fire alarm, push on parked cars in case any alarms go off, but keep moving and behind some sort of protective screen. Get to other people. Don't yell *help*, yell *fire!* Either you escape or the guy gets closer, in which case, keep reading.
2. The guy is across the room from you (about ten to twelve feet away). This is a gun's most effective range. Toss him your wallet or the keys to your car, whatever he wants. Either he takes your wallet and keys and goes away, or he moves closer to you, in which case, keep reading.
3. The guy has the gun up against you. If you think he is probably not going to shoot you, just comply as necessary. And if I may make a policy statement here, it is better to be robbed or even raped than dead. If you disagree, fine. You die.

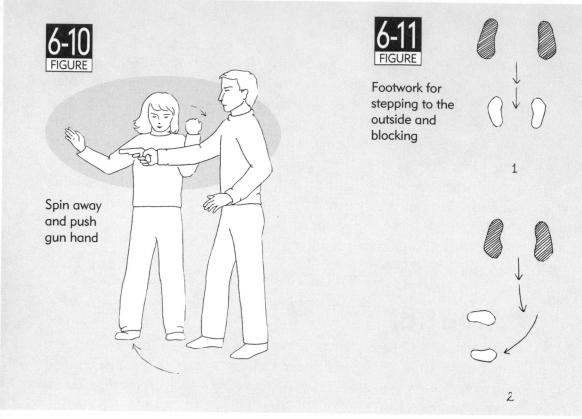

6-10
FIGURE

Spin away and push gun hand

6-11
FIGURE

Footwork for stepping to the outside and blocking

1

2

In the event that you think you will be shot even if you comply, and you have nothing to lose, then you must appear to be as compliant as possible. Raise your hands, saying, "Please don't shoot; I'll cooperate." Yes, you're lying, but so what, I forgive you. Then, even as you are speaking, move. Spin out to your right and knock the gun away to your left, or vice versa (Figure 6-10). It doesn't matter which direction you spin in as long as you push the gun the other way; although if you have time to think about it, spin to the outside of the attacker. The principle is that you move two things—both your body and the attacker's arm (Figure 6-11).

Try to block so that your forearm or hand comes in contact with the attacker's hand, or as close to it as possible. As soon as the gun is no longer pointing in your direction, you can choose to follow up with a kick to the knees or a poke to the eyes or throat—any damaging strike that comes to mind. Improvise possibilities with your partner.

This is yet another place where your wrist-lock practice will serve you in good stead. Try the following:

Immediately after you spin outside and block, clamp down with your left hand over the top (thumb side) of the hand holding the gun

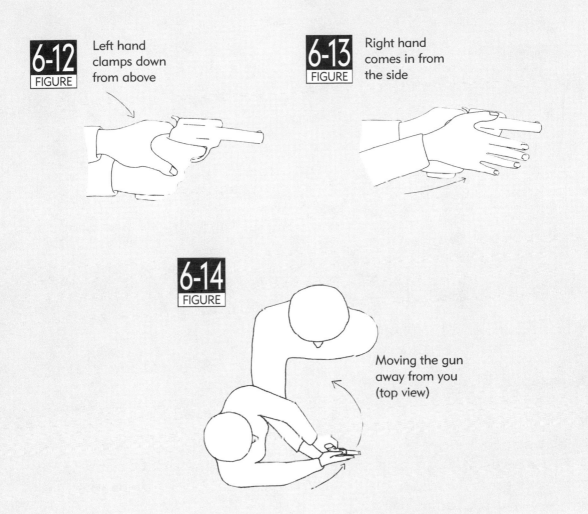

6-12 FIGURE Left hand clamps down from above

6-13 FIGURE Right hand comes in from the side

6-14 FIGURE

Moving the gun away from you (top view)

(Figure 6-12). Bring the palm of your right hand, fingers pointing along the barrel of the gun, flat against the back of the hand holding the gun (Figure 6-13). Practice this until you can do it very quickly and smoothly: spin out, clamp down and palm in.

Now you are standing to the side of your partner, with both your hands controlling the weapon. Remember, all of you is now fighting one small part of your attacker.

Apply pressure with both of your hands so that the barrel of the gun moves in a horizontal arc away from you and around toward your attacker (Figure 6-14). Do this in a quick, fluid motion, letting your hips and feet drive the movement. You will find that there will come a point where, due to your leverage on the gun itself as well as on the attacker's wrist, your attacker is forced to relinquish the weapon

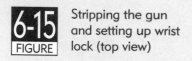

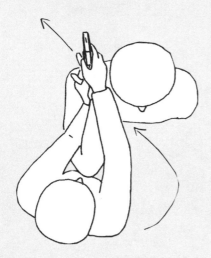

(Figure 6-15). It is a simple matter to strip it from his hand. Of course, his finger in the trigger guard could get badly mangled; be careful with your practice partner.

However, you should understand that fighting is an untidy business where absolutely anything can happen. Even if he does not release the gun for some reason, you are now in an excellent position to continue to apply pressure to the wrist, locking it out completely and thereby bringing your attacker onto his back on the floor (Figure 6-16).

It's not perfect, and you should never try to be a hero. You would only do something this foolhardy if it was the only option open other than getting shot. You could still get shot—it's just preferable to maybe get shot than to definitely get shot. When a guy has a gun at you, none of your options are necessarily good; some are just less bad.

As you may remember from waaaay back in the introduction, I've been held up at close-range gunpoint twice, and meek compliance was all that was required. Thank Zeus.

In Closing

The only further advice I can give you is to repeat everything I said in the beginning. Don't be stupid. If you are attacked, fight like a tiger and don't let up. Practice all your techniques, from the most basic falling down (I can do that!) to the most sophisticated, exquisitely painful joint locks. In fact, don't let a week go by without a practice session.

Remember your weapons: hands, feet, elbows, knees, and fingernails. The floor is a weapon. Leverage and momentum are weapons. Surprise is a weapon; the bad guy picked you to attack because he thought he would win. When you fight back, instantly and with ferocity, in that moment you have the advantage.

If you are dumb enough to pick a fight with a bigger, stronger, meaner person, you may still lose. You're not Wonder Woman—but you don't have to be to defend yourself.

Information is your most important weapon. Don't let fear get in your way of having a life. When I suggest that you walk down the street thinking of what you would use as a weapon if someone suddenly leapt out at you, it in no way indicates that I think this is likely. I have trained in martial arts for many years and have never yet had to use my fighting skills anywhere out of the practice hall or the tournament ring. I'm not afraid to admit this, and I don't think it impinges on my credentials in any way. Heck, my obstetrician was a guy. Think about it.

Now you know something about fighting. If you want to go further than the material presented here, find a good martial arts school near you. Choose one that is easy to get to, has classes at the hours that you are likely to attend, and a teacher who presents material in a way that feels comfortable and respectful. There are a lot of great dojos across the country, and some very wonderful and informative self defense courses, too. A book like this is a useful tool, but it is certainly not the only tool.

Keep practicing!

Index

About the Author

In search of exercise with a plot as well as cheap therapy, the author found martial arts to be in curious harmony with her Quaker roots. ("Friend, if thee doesn't move, I will put my fist where thee is standing.") She studies Shaolin Kempo Karate in the Boston area, and has received her third-degree black belt.

For more information, or to order, call 800-872-5627 or visit www.adamsmedia.com/everything

Adams Media Corporation, 260 Center Street, Holbrook, MA 02343